LEAVING ROOM FOR HOPE

LEAVING ROOM

FOR HOPE

SERMONS FOR UNCERTAIN TIMES

Judith E. Meyer
Minister
Unitarian Universalist Community Church
Santa Monica, California

Foreword by
Ernest D. Pipes, Jr.
Minister Emeritus

Edited by
Felicity A. Nussbaum

KayT Publishing
Long Beach, California

Judith E. Meyer

Leaving Room for Hope: Sermons for Uncertain Times

Published by KayT Publishing
Long Beach, California

ISBN 0-971-6565-3-3

TO THE CONGREGATION

TABLE OF CONTENTS

ACKNOWLEDGMENTS

This collection of sermons would not have happened if Felicity Nussbaum had not offered to serve as editor, publisher, and mentor. I have no idea how she found the time for this project, but I shall always be grateful that she did.

The cover drawing is by David Denton. He drew it while we were in Marrakesh during my sabbatical. I never would have gotten there without him.

Ernie Pipes graciously agreed to write the Foreword. No publication about our church would be complete without his presence. His ministry and character are an inspiration for me.

Thank you to Luther Nussbaum and his publishing house; and to Joyce Lee, who helped with the formatting of the manuscript, unseen but essential support for this project.

The Reverend Judith E. Meyer
February, 2006

FOREWORD

In the Sunday morning hour, the sermon is but one segment in a rich and colorful collage comprised of instrumental and choral music, congregational singing, readings, and various ceremonies and celebrations in which the congregation participates. Nevertheless, in the Protestant tradition, the pulpit is the center of focus and the sermon (the message for the morning) is the centerpiece and sets the theme which brings all the other elements of the hour together. The sermon title and topic are published in advance, and its subject frequently is what fills the pews.

The traditional sermon had a text, invariably drawn from the Bible, and its intent was to lift from the text its moral and spiritual wisdom and apply these teachings to the everyday lives of the people. The sermon was essentially a teaching instrument and, as such, drew upon the preacher's personal experiences, vivid illustrations, humor, inspirational stories; and, if the preacher was gifted, the sermon could also display considerable literary merit.

Today, in our Unitarian Universalist congregations, while the sermon still can be measured against most of these qualities, its resources and purposes are greatly broadened. As the banners on the sanctuary wall demonstrate, we gladly draw upon all the great wisdom traditions of humankind. And while the sermon may teach in the sense of opening the mind to new ideas, it may also address personal problems and social ills of many kinds. Its purpose may be to lift us toward broader visions of life that we tend to overlook in our everyday rush, to illuminate ways of living that manifest love of all earth's creatures and invite wonder and reverence before the mystery of the creation. Sermons can be designed to inspire commitment to justice and non-violence in the affairs of individuals and nations and to imbue a hunger to experience first hand the many splendors of the good, the true, and the beautiful.

And if you, over time, become a connoisseur of sermons, you will notice that there is a "preaching year"--a kind of liturgical calendar that asks "What time is it in our lives?" The preaching calendar celebrates the festivals of spring, summer, autumn, and winter with their special joys. In addition, there are pastoral sermons that address issues of relationships, ethical behavior, how to make it through the week. And there are prophetic sermons that challenge us to social witness, to work for peace and justice. As pastoral sermons "comfort the afflicted," prophetic sermons "afflict the comfortable." And there are sermons of "institutional reform and renewal"--for the church is not a static thing but must change and grow if it is to creatively serve a vital congregation. And of course, every sermon is inescapably autobiographical, revealing the life experiences, feelings, values and convictions of the person who dares to occupy a pulpit. The preacher, like the harpist, has many strings to play across the year if those in the pews are to be touched in deep places and their lives in some measure healed and transformed. For attempting this is the essence of ministry.

The pages which follow marvelously exhibit all these homiletic powers, and many more. Judith is particularly gifted at sharing the hard-earned wisdom of her life and the beauty of her spirit. But by reading these sermons you will not reap the full benefit of hearing them; her voice, pulpit style and presence are, alas, not fully transferable into print. So why not join me in the pews some Sunday morning?

The Reverend Ernie Pipes, Minister Emeritus
Unitarian Universalist Community Church of Santa Monica

PREFACE

I write sermons, a traditional form of communication that is primarily oral. I preach before a congregation that gathers week after week, in the same sanctuary, among friends and strangers, conscious of our collective strengths, weaknesses, histories, and foibles. What happens in the sermon has something to do with relationship, with self-disclosure, and with intimacy. In many ways it is a mystery to me.

Although my sermons are often personal, or pertain to some specific aspect of the life of my community, I always try to make the connection to some larger, more universal aspect of human experience. This is how I understand my relationship to God and why I share my experience with others. Even if I am talking about myself, I hope they are hearing something about themselves.

The sermons in this collection are arranged under categories that have some spiritual meaning for me. My spiritual practice is grounded in everyday life. When I render it into words to be spoken to others, I discover the sacredness of life for myself.

The Reverend Judith E. Meyer
Santa Monica, California

EDITOR'S COMMENT

It seems ironic in a time when the world is being ripped apart along religious lines that it is so hard to find the literature of faith. Fear and its accompanying anxiety are much easier to locate than faith. The sermons of the Reverend Judith Meyer included here speak with reason, passion, and conviction to troubled spirits in modern times. She speaks in a personal voice that reflects anxieties about a world in crisis. It is a voice that engages fully with that anxiety on a personal and intellectual level, yet these words also soothe those who listen to it. Why, these meditations ask, has the pervasiveness of spirituality not made the world a more humane place? What gives our anxious lives meaning? In defining anxiety as authenticity, Judith Meyer elevates the path of seeking comfort to one that is essential to leading a life of integrity.

Rooted in the everyday and the ordinary, Judith Meyer draws on common occurrences and experiences--learning the alphabet, walking the dog, going to the hardware store, rowing a boat--to write about larger, abstract, and even universal matters with compassion and understanding. These mundane activities teach deeper meanings. Searching for the right drain cleaner subtly evolves into a lesson in forging human bonds. The gentle absurdity of having one's dog mistaken for a film star relieves grief. The demanding perfectionism of a beloved father transforms itself into a lesson in the difficulty of shaping our own image of the divine. Falling into the murky Santa Monica Bay while learning to maneuver a boat, she leads us to accept the comedy of miscalculation and exult in the joy of achievement. The words included here also testify poignantly to the loneliness that is Los Angeles, but they quickly turn to the more pervasive loneliness of urban living everywhere, and beyond that to the modern condition of feeling isolated from each other. From the darkness of that loneliness Judith Meyer teases out the potential for freedom and faith, and for the unexpected thrill of beauty or community.

A word about the way that the sermons appear on the page: in their original form, they are reminiscent of poetry, designed to slow the reader down, and to imitate the deliberate cadences of the spoken word. Here all but the first sermon have been condensed into paragraph form for easier reading. These talks, originally written to be delivered in a particular place and on a particular occasion, derive from the Unitarian Universalist tradition of thought, but they are not limited by dogma. A principled and progressive faith, it reveals "an individual truth that reminds us we are not alone," as Judith puts it. It is one which draws from the spiritual strength of Native American knowledge, Hindu ritual, Jewish wisdom, Christian scripture, Zen meditation, and Islamic history. It encompasses thinking as wide as the folksy wisdom of Jean Shepherd, the esoteric thought of William James, and the insights of feminism. But its eclecticism is thoughtful rather than random. As she demonstrates with humor and clarity, the intellectual path is not a sufficient avenue to faith.

Both believers and nonbelievers share personal struggles and anxious times. These talks wrestle with the difficult task of living a meaningful life, and of finding a center when chaos threatens everywhere, especially in a post-September 11 world. The sermons speak of the *search* for belief, though the nature of that belief is an evolving and questioning one. The concept of pilgrimage seems to take on new relevance when we awaken to the possibility of finding something or someone that transforms us through contact with the wondrous or the holy. Through Judith Meyer's words of hope, the spiritual quest is revealed as a way to become whole, and even to offset hostile and destructive forces in modern society. They steadily encourage us in the quest to find personal and global peace. The untidy and confusing path to faith challenges us to learn to forge connections, to rejoice in being alive, and to shape a productive life against all odds.

Felicity A. Nussbaum
Santa Monica, California

LEAVING ROOM FOR HOPE

LEAVING ROOM FOR HOPE

August 28, 2005

I'm about to leave this pulpit--
>and all my work here--
>>for a four-month sabbatical.
It seems only right to take the time
>to talk to you about what I will be doing
>>while I'm away.
My main project will be
>to put together a collection of my sermons.
I'll also be taking a trip to Morocco.
I'm sure I'll have something to say
>about visiting a Muslim country
>>when I come back.
But the main product of my time off will be a book.

As Donald Hall notes,
>writers work alone,
>>and so do I--
>>>at least when I'm sitting at my desk.
But I am never really alone
>when I write sermons.

You are always with me.

I think of sermons as letters to my congregation,

    often imagining

        how you might respond

            to what I have to say.

I won't be working alone on this book either.

Church member Felicity Nussbaum,

    who also happens to be a professor of English at UCLA,

        is helping me.

Actually, this book was her idea.

She offered to edit--

    and publish--

        my work.

All I have to do is select forty-seven sermons.

At first she said forty,

    but somewhere along the line she raised my quota.

So far I have sent her twenty-one.

Last June,

    our church archivist, Rob Briner,

        dropped off at my home

            two large file boxes of my sermons.

Between what's in these boxes

    and what is stored on my hard drive

        is work that spans twelve years now.

I have been going back through the years
and reading all of it.

I'm not as prolific or talented a writer as Donald Hall,
      but I do understand how it feels
            to read my own work many years later.
"Then I remember,"
      Hall writes,
         "sagging suddenly,
            heavy as mud,
               black, and hopeless …
when I have come later to realize
      that the words I wrote with such excitement
         were nothing, nothing at all …"
My writing makes me cringe.
Oh, I might finish off a sermon on a Saturday afternoon,
      and carried away by my own rhetoric,
         feel pretty good;
            even excited.
Depending on how it goes over Sunday morning,
      I might be able to keep that feeling up for a while.
But the shelf life of sermons is miserably short.
Especially if they're mine.
"Did I really say that?"
      I ask myself,
         ten years later.

And the titles are of two kinds:

    the grim, existentialist ones like "Leaving Room for Hope,"

        or to reprise a couple of my greatest hits,

           "Blessed are the Depressed"

              and "The Illusion of a Future."

They don't promise much of an uplift;

    I'm sorry.

All the rest have either the word "spirit" or "faith" in them,

    so that you know you are in church.

Try taking this material and organizing it

    into something coherent.

That's Felicity's job.

I just churn it out.

You can see why

    I've never thought about writing a book before.

I don't like working with my own words

    once I've spoken them.

I love writing sermons,

    and I've learned to enjoy preaching them.

But I'm a harsh critic.

I rarely look back.

Mercifully I forget what I've preached

    by the Monday after.

But you don't.

Some of you remember my sermons better than I do.

I am touched by that.

Getting started on this project

    has renewed my awareness of just how interactive

        sermon-writing is.

Yes, I sit alone at my desk for one day each week,

    undergoing my own personal creative panic,

        and delivering,

            by Sunday morning,

                something I have fashioned just for you.

I can't imagine writing for strangers.

I want you to know that.

So this project is a collaborative one,

    and you and Felicity and I are all involved,

        along with a couple of my demons,

            and we'll see how far we go in four months.

This book is also a once in a lifetime experience for me.

It is an honor to work with Felicity,

    who is an author and distinguished scholar.

And it is an opportunity

    to create something

        for which there is virtually no market.

Except for all of you,
> of course.

We're going to mark up the price,
> sell the books to church members,
>> and give the money to the building program.

Books of sermons represent the life work
> of a minister and congregation.

They are a glimpse of the relationship
> and the time we have shared together.

In this sense they are specific and precious.

I feel some pressure
> to make this collection my very best,
>> because it is probably all that will remain
>>> of my work after I am gone.

Well, there will also be the archives,
> which have been so carefully organized
> and tended by Rob.

No book can capture a life work,
> especially work that is as varied and challenging as ministry.

Only part of what I do involves writing.

I want my book to be a testament to ministry,
> not just a sample of my writing.

I want to create something

that says,

    "here I stand;

        this is what I have to give."

I want to do this just as we all do.

Every one of us has life work.

And it means the same thing,

    whatever that work is.

I keep a tattered index card

    in the hymn book I use at my desk.

Written on the card are words by Ernest Becker,

    a mid-twentieth century writer most famous for his great work,

        The Denial of Death.

He wrote,

"Who knows what form the forward momentum of life will take

    or what use it will make

        of our anguished searching.

The most any of us can seem to do

    is to fashion something--

        an object or ourselves--

            and drop it into the confusion,

                make an offering of it,

                    so to speak,

                        to the life force."

This is our life work:

> to make an offering of ourselves,

>> to give back to the force that made us.

This offering is unlimited in its variety.

Whether you are a teacher or parent,

> an artist, musician, or craftsperson,

>> a scholar or an activist,

>>> a healer or caregiver,

>>>> whether you support or lead,

>>>>> serve or direct,

>>>>>> you have something to

>>>>>>> give back.

If you don't find that something on the job,

> you find it at home,

>> or here,

>>> or somewhere only you know--

>>>> but you find it.

As Ernest Becker admits,

> it may involve some anguished searching.

Yet it is what is ultimately powerful and life-affirming

> about this human condition we share.

We can make something of ourselves

> and give it back.

These things we make do not last long.

It's a rare work of art that doesn't get lost

in the onward rush of time.

But in a way,

    that is why we feel the need

        to make something.

We need to make a gesture towards transcendence,

    even if it lasts only a little longer

        than we do.

While Donald Hall was writing his book *Life Work*,

    he learned that he had a recurrence of cancer.

"When I went into the hospital,"

    he writes,

        "I brought work with me,

            and in the last two days before I went home

            I started writing again."

"When I began to recover,"

    he continues,

"still anxious about recurrence,

    I worked with a manic prolixity--

        not well--

            and knew in my heart

                that I worked against death.

What's more,

    I realized that I had always worked--

        the real thing, the absorbedness--

            in defiance of death."

Our life work--

    the thing we fashion out of ourselves--

        is not only a gift to the life force.

It is the only thing we have

    to face down death.

It is how we overcome oblivion:

    with the full force of our being

        we generate our own moment of transcendence

        while we can.

I decided to call this book of mine *Leaving Room for Hope*,

    because ministry has taught me

        that despite everything--

            death and oblivion,

failure and disappointment,

    and the futility of holding on to anything or anyone,

        there is something we can--

        and should--do.

There is always a way

    we can take the full force of our being,

        and "drop it into the confusion,"

            as Becker sees it.

And we can trust that this tiny gesture

    is how we prevail,

        in the face of all that dooms us;

            our small but powerful testament

to the life force

   and our token of gratitude for its gift.

Thank you for this gift of time,

   for your presence in my life work,

      and for the faith we share.

Resources used to prepare this sermon include Ernest Becker, *The Denial of Death* (New York: The Free Press, 1973), and Donald Hall, *Life Work* (Boston: Beacon Press, 1993).

WHY I PRAY

November 5, 2000

Religious liberals have sought diligently for years to find fresh and relevant definitions of prayer. Bishop John Shelby Spong makes a passionate appeal in his book for prayer as the exercise of an authentic life. "Prayer is what I am doing," he writes, "when I live wastefully, passionately, and wondrously and invite others to do so with me or even because of me." More practical, perhaps, is the definition we find in our covenant:

> Love is the doctrine of this church.
> The quest of truth is its sacrament,
>   and *service* is its prayer."

This perspective is consistent with the Unitarian Universalist emphasis on deeds, not creeds, as the standard of the good life. We are at our best when we are acting on our principles. The liberal religious understanding of prayer as authentic living or service to others is an honest attempt to recast traditional religious forms in the terms of contemporary experience. We do not offer prayers "by storming the gates of heaven," nor do we imagine our God as residing there. For Bishop Spong, prayer is the here and now experience of coming fully alive. "There is only the call to be open to the depths of life," he writes, "and to live in such a way as to reveal those depths."

Bishop Spong continues, "I do not believe that there is a being, a supernatural deity, standing over against my world who seeks through some invasive process to imprint the divine will on the life of my world. The deity I worship," he adds, "is rather part of who I am individually and corporately.... God is the presence in whom my being comes alive." I do not believe in a supernatural deity either. I'm not pinning my hopes on the "everlasting arms" that may or may not be waiting to catch me when I fall.

But like Bishop Spong, I do have a sense of God, not the God of theism or the bible, but a sense of something holy, which I still seek, however tentatively, to be part of my life. And prayer is my appeal to that God or that "something holy" to enter my life and even to change it. This is the culmination, if you can call it that, of the years I have spent contemplating, rejecting, and revising my image of God. As those of you who have children are frequently reminded, this thinking starts early in all of us. When I was very young, I had many fervent religious interests and tried everything from devotional rituals to giving up listening to my transistor radio for Lent, as a way of seeking God. My parents tolerated my preoccupations with good humor and little comprehension. I asked my father if he believed in God. "I worship Apollo," he told me, and then directed me to read all of Bulfinch's *Mythology*. They were good Unitarian Universalist parents, but they tried too hard to intellectualize religion and left me looking on my own for spiritual experiences. They think that is why I became a minister.

My childhood image of God as the object of devotion soon gave way to God as an intellectual exercise when I studied philosophy in college. There is nothing quite as effective for losing faith in God as studying proofs of His existence! Once I made it to Hegel and then on to Marx, Heidegger and the existentialists, I never looked back. I became convinced that the human enterprise was tragic, that the only authentic state was anxiety, and we could save ourselves only by facing up to this bleak reality. After a while, I cheered up, and wondered whether God might have something to do with life *not* always being tragic and occasionally offering some relief instead of dread. Whatever this glimmer of hope and transcendence might be, I was willing to call it God, and today I still do. It's just a glimmer, but the light stays on.

My sense of God has changed throughout my life, as I imagine it has for you, and yet something I've noticed is that my use of prayer has hardly changed at all. I admire the liberal religious view of prayer as service, or social action, or celebration, or any of the ways in which we are at our best, but that's not how I pray. I don't pray often. But when I do, it's because I'm desperate.

I want to tell you about this, because sometimes these prayers, desperate though they may have been, have changed my life. Not because they were answered in any obvious way. Not because the universe offered me any signs to confirm that I was going in the right direction. Not because of anything outside myself, actually--but because of something inside, something that allowed me to open up, or to change, or to move on in ways I desperately needed to do.

I have prayed for sleep. I have prayed for forgiveness. I have prayed when I've had it with my perfectionism and need help with acceptance. I have prayed for healing. I have prayed for people I know who are suffering. I have prayed by hospital bedsides when there is nothing left to say. And I have prayed when I feel cut off from the spirit of life, when I feel trapped, no longer in touch with my own true self.

Our story for the children this morning was a mystical narrative in which the Maasai man sings to the spirits of the animals caged in the zoo. They get a glimmering of something that reminds them of who they really are, and they don't feel sad and trapped anymore. When they remember their own true selves, they feel free. Prayer is like the song of the Maasai man. It can rekindle the awareness of who we really are, and remind us of the spirit within. We can turn to it when we feel trapped too, held back by our own limitations and weaknesses, or frustrated by the constraints our lives have imposed on us, or when we have nowhere else to turn.

The best advice anyone ever gave me about prayer was this: just ask for what you want. Just ask: not because you will receive, but because there is hope and healing in naming what you want. There is hope and healing in the truth, whatever the outcome you seek. Mary Oliver writes,

> [And] if your spirit carries within it
> the thorn that is heavier than lead--
> if it's all you can do to keep on trudging--
> there is still somewhere deep within you
> a beast shouting that the earth
> is exactly what it wanted.

These words are for those of us who have felt the pain of not being exactly who we wanted to be; and for those who have had to hoist the heavier burdens of life: illness, disappointment, loss; and also for those of us whose personal struggles are mundane but no less tragic or impenetrable. For any of us, the thorn can become heavier than lead at any time. When it does, there is still the beast deep within, still shouting, still living in the spirit of what is light, natural and free. That is where prayer can lead, if we let it take us there.

Prayer is primitive and fundamental. It is the naked recognition of who we are and what we want. Prayer is speaking the truth to ourselves, not always an easy thing to do. We express ourselves in our most vulnerable state. Perhaps that is why people have sent their prayers to heaven: far away, safely out of reach. But what we need is what *can* reach us: to sense the spirit within, and know the truth of ourselves. The truth is what can reach us. Prayer is letting it find us. Once we know the truth, we are free to change and grow and find what we are seeking in life.

We religious liberals are skeptical about prayer because we reject the materialism of asking for something we want, and we lack the belief in a supernatural agent to provide it. But asking for what we need, whether that is the strength to change and grow, or the courage to face our fears, or the willingness to move closer to others--asking is the first step towards finding what we need, and becoming the agents of our own true selves. In this sense, we pray to the spirit within us that helps us to move in the direction we desire. As Bishop Spong says, "There is no magic here!" There may even be no God here, just the human yearning to live honestly and to be true to oneself.

I still pray to God, because if I need to pray badly enough, I don't have time to define and qualify what I mean. But if I were to define and qualify what I mean, I would say that God is the spirit at the center of life in which I place my trust and my vulnerability. Something like that. Bishop Spong's definition works well too: "God is the presence in whom my being comes alive."

But you don't need God to pray. You only need your true self, and a willingness to open your true self to your deepest yearnings, hopes, and fears. Whatever you have is enough.

I also want to tell you my one other belief about prayer. When my prayers are answered, I give thanks. I try never to forget to give thanks. It may be some imaginary transaction going on in my head, but it does not feel complete to me until I have acknowledged my gratitude for whatever I have received. Perhaps I'm relieved that whatever crisis provoked the prayer is over.

Or I realize one day that something has changed in me and that I have grown in some way I really needed to do. Or I think about my life and feel grateful. I give thanks. And then I move on, no longer as heavy as lead, more in touch with my true self, knowing, at least for that moment, that something holy goes with me too and is never too far away.

Resources used to prepare this sermon include Laura Berkeley, *The Spirit of the Maasai Man* (New York: Barefoot Books, 2000); John Shelby Spong, *Why Christianity Must Change or Die* (New York: HarperCollins Publishers, 1998); and Mary Oliver, "Morning Poem" in *New and Selected Poems* (Boston: Beacon Press, 1992).

MORE KIND THAN HOME, MORE LARGE THAN EARTH

Delivered at the UUA General Assembly

June 22, 2001

"Something has spoken to me in the night, burning the tapers of the waning year ...." When Thomas Wolfe wrote these words he was still a young man. And though he did not know it, he would die before long, too. An intuitive sense of his fate may have lent urgency to his work, for *You Can't Go Home Again* was nothing less than a voluminous outpouring of commentary on the human condition. The book was not published until after his death.

Wolfe had a sharp eye on reality; his voyeuristic observations nailed what is twisted, hypocritical and vain in human nature. But he also expressed a belief in another reality, transcendent and true, for which he held out hope and a shred of innocent longing. Try to imagine, Wolfe suggested, what would happen if we were to let go of all that holds us to places, people, life itself--to lose everything, and leave everyone--try to imagine what would be left.

Perhaps Wolfe was simply telling us that after we die, we go to a place like that--and it's a better place than earth, and our better selves will feel at home at last. Even so, it's not a conventional image of heaven, because this one is connected to the earth. It is a place, Wolfe says,

> Whereon the pillars of this earth are founded,
> Toward which the conscience of the world is tending--
> A wind is rising, and the rivers flow.

We have a sense of this land "more kind than home" from what we see here on earth every day. The "conscience of the world" assures us it is there. Nature itself flows towards it.

What better affirmation can any of us make, if not that somewhere at the end of all our struggle and effort, there is a place we can envision. It resolves the injustices and contradictions of our human ways, and it forgives what went wrong and it keeps what is good; a place that is not really a place at all, but a moral role in creation, that heals divisions and stands for some great benevolent truth we know in our hearts is real.

Not that any of us this is easy to express. Especially for us-- having solidly anchored ourselves in the day-to-day imperatives of our faith, the work of community and service and education--we leave the question of a larger reality unsettled, since we are not the ones to settle it. So many of us have had to strip away layers of indoctrination from experiences of religion earlier in life, we welcome the expansive, open sense of not knowing, and it makes us feel free.

Our own faith makes no demands on us to seek or express our sense of God, or what love may hold us in its embrace as we go about our days. Thomas Wolfe talks about it in different ways: that land more kind than home, which calls forth so many associations; a place more large than earth, which looks towards all creation; and yet, despite the power of these images, they describe little. What they do instead is stir the heart to hope and to faith that a good life is worth living; that nothing is wasted, and no one is lost, in that land more kind than home, more large than earth.

Recently a family called me to visit a dying man. He was not a Unitarian Universalist. His only connection with our faith was that he visited a UU church in New York City with friends from time to time. When he learned that he was to die soon, everyone, including him, seemed to think that he needed a minister. Not knowing any, they remembered their visits to the church in New York, and called me. Such encounters put our own faith to the test. We put such value on our relatedness, the sharing of ourselves, the intimacy of our community life. We know each other. Our ministry is an extension of that familiarity.

But I was invited to sit in a room with a stranger. I knew a little about him. I knew that he had cast off his Episcopalian upbringing. There might be something he wanted to confess. We talked about some of his unfinished life work, and the status of his relationships. And then we sat together for the longest time. A few more halting attempts to open up possible areas of concern led us to talk about what happens when we die.

We Unitarian Universalists don't talk about such things much, and when we do, we don't agree. But I wasn't there to give him a survey of UU attitudes about life after death, and it occurred to me at that moment how utterly useless such self-inventories are. All I had to offer him were my own tentative thoughts, the only ones I could speak with any authority, not that they were based on anything but my individual, rather primitive beliefs.

I said to him, "Well, I've always thought--ever since I was a young child, that there is some part of us that belongs to God. And I think that part of us existed before we were born and goes on after we die. And I imagine that when we die, we don't go on consciously as the person we were in life," and when I said that, I cringed a little, for this man had one day, at most, left to be himself: "I imagine that something does survive, and that we follow it, or become it, and it takes us home."

It's amazing what comes out of us when we are confronted with the exigency of a situation such as this. More than anything, I felt I needed to speak the truth as I understood it. And I needed that truth to be something that would comfort, not anger, or frighten, a man who was about to lose the only life he had.

"To lose the earth you know, for greater knowing, but lose the life you have, for greater life, to leave the friends you loved, for greater loving...." Can any one of us be in the presence of death and not reach for the greater knowing, the greater life, the greater loving that some part of us insists is real and will sustain us, come what may? I can't.

I came home from my visit with the dying man. The phone rang. "He wants to see you again," his wife said. "Come tomorrow." But the next day he was gone. Since then I've thought a lot about our faith and what its message has to give to the world. Much of what we have to say speaks from our tradition of individualism, which has taught us the values of diversity and tolerance. In these values we see freedom and growth. As A. Powell Davies said, our faith "begins with individual freedom of belief." Some people think God wears a blue hat--to recall Christopher Buice's fable--and some thinks she wears a red one. Some think that God really doesn't exist at all.

In Buice's story, the people get so incensed over their differences that they split down the middle and build a wall to stay away from each other. Not until God herself comes back one day and sees what they have done do they learn that God can wear a hat that is blue and red, if she wants to. And they wake up to the truth that these differences between us do not matter at all. What matters is enjoying each other and tearing down the walls that keep us apart.

Our faith tradition has long preoccupied itself with honoring difference. And that is a large part of who we are, learning what it means to be in community with some who see red hats, and others who see blue hats. But we sometimes appear to have forgotten that our Unitarian and Universalist faiths have also pointed to something beyond difference, to something beyond Unitarianism and Universalism even, to something we cannot capture or define, yet is our hope and our truth. It is something that "goes out to the limitless," as Davies said, the transcendent reality that is "more large than earth," where walls come down, "more kind than home," where God helps people enjoy life--and each other. Our hope and our truth are to be whole, not divided; to find the place of greater life, and greater love, and to make our home there, together. There the wind is rising and the rivers flow, and the conscience of the world is tending. There we know our soul's true self, in the eternal flow of life, where all are free and we are one.

Resources used to prepare this sermon include A. Powell Davies, *The Faith of an Unrepentant Liberal* (Washington, D.C.: All Souls Church, Unitarian, 1946); Christopher Buice, "God's Hat" in *A Bucketful of Dreams: Contemporary Parables for All Ages* (Boston: Skinner House, 1995); and Thomas Wolfe, *You Can't Go Home Again* (New York: Harper & Row, 1934).

ACCEPTANCE

September 20, 1998

Modern moral advice offers a bracing direction to today's seekers: change what you can and accept the rest, powerful help that has saved many from self-destruction and despair. Neither advice is easy to follow. Whether you're committed to a twelve-step program or engaged in uphill social activism, change is consuming and difficult to achieve. Still, change brings with it a desirable outcome, a sense of accomplishment. Acceptance requires us to yield to inert realities, our will a useless force. Though we may all agree we need acceptance to live at peace with ourselves; and acknowledge, even, that life goes on whether we accept it or not; we still trouble our souls with incessant maneuvers to keep acceptance far, far away.

When Spalding Gray decided that he wanted, desperately, to win a role in the film *The Killing Fields*, he walked away from his interview poorly prepared to accept any outcome but the one he desired. What resulted was a sojourn in the realm of magical thinking and compulsion, which produced a comic narrative, but must have been--and would have been for any of us--a painful and bewildering experience. Eventually arriving at the conclusion that no matter how contrived, his antics would not guarantee his success, Gray gave up, and came up with a new sense of his power, though equally deluded, and moved on.

Spalding Gray's story gives us an image of the futility--and the humanness--of striving to control realities that are beyond our control. But having given up control does not mean that we have no power. For in the realm of letting go and finding acceptance, we may discover power we did not know we had.

A colleague once gave me some very good advice. When she must do something she does not want to do, she told me, she gives herself a moment to let go--she described it as saying a prayer of letting go--and then proceeds with her obligation. This obvious bit of information has helped me more than I can say. You see, before she told me about letting go, I would run through my mind every imaginable fantasy about how I could get out of whatever it was I was supposed to do. Then, still fantasizing and struggling with my obligation, I would grudgingly go and do what I did not want to do, most likely to no one's benefit. I never let go. Coming home, I'd still be complaining to myself about what a horrific experience I just had. I never let go.

After realizing how valuable my colleague's advice was, I began to practice letting go before doing something I resisted. I didn't pray, rather I would announce to myself, "I am now letting go," and--admittedly, I would often have to do this more than once--it would work. Whatever happened next felt somehow free of struggle, turning out, often enough, to be enjoyable or rewarding in some surprising way. Letting go gave me the power to participate fully in whatever came next.

We rarely hasten to let go, and our hesitation is often for very good reason. Great moral gains have resulted from some tenacious visionary refusing to let go of the dream of some new justice. The leader whose work we praise and credit for moving humanity forward--a Gandhi or a King--carried on despite huge obstacles. Their moral imagination and vision incubated in the realm between change and letting go--and they allied themselves on the side of change. They were right.

Sometimes we are wrong. Learning when to work for change and when to let go is a worthy human dilemma, perhaps one for which we are uniquely suited. In his latest book *Consilience,* biologist E.O. Wilson offers a view of the human mind that explains why we never seem to know when to stop. The brain is a machine assembled not to understand itself, but to survive, Wilson writes. Everything that we know and can ever know about existence is both stimulated and limited by our mental processes. We do not need to know much to survive as a species, but we are endowed with just enough extra capacity to keep learning and growing, living on the adaptive edge of evolution, though with not enough to understand it. Not knowing may even keep us moving forward.

Wilson's view of humanity is original and bold. What it helps us see is that acceptance is not part of our nature--but pushing against it is. Knowing just a little bit more than we need to survive drives the cycles of life itself, and who knows, we may come to know just exactly what they are someday.

For tireless scientists like Wilson, acceptance is neither a spiritual value nor a glimmering of mysteries we were not meant to understand. It is the wall we hit when our brains can take us no further. Human dignity takes over then, and we graciously yield our inquiry to the next generation. On a scale considerably smaller than evolutionary time, however, each of us individuals will need to learn acceptance at critical stages of life. Sometimes willfully summoning it, other times graciously--or awkwardly--yielding to it, the cycles of our lives lead us back and forth, pushing against and bowing humbly before our limits. If we have to do it, and we do, there's some comfort in doing it together. The need to accept many realities, some harsher than others, hovers over a community like ours at all times, and especially right now.

In a church we are always conscious of death and the life cycles that bring us through the stages of being human in the midst of much we cannot change. At the same time, our temperaments lean towards activism, and our appetites crave more knowledge. Not all the tasks of being human merge into a neat, livable formula. Sometimes we bumble forward, learning only afterward what our experience meant, if it meant anything at all. The last time I told you about an experience I had in London when I was a teenager wandering around there alone, I can still remember your blank uncomprehending faces trying to understand what point I was trying to make by telling you about this. This is one of those life experiences I just can't forget, or stop talking about, even though I may eventually have to accept that it has no meaning to others, let go, and give it up. I tell it because it helps me remember that there is comfort in people acknowledging to each other that there are some things we simply must accept--unknowns, mysteries or uncharted scientific territory, it makes no difference what they are--but we somehow do better if we're not in it all alone.

In the summer of 1969, I was traveling through the British Isles, wandering restlessly through cities and towns. I may have been on some ill-defined quest that led me occasionally into a concert hall or museum, but I've never been an adventurous traveler, and most of the time I felt lost and unhinged. Too proud to go home, I took up sitting in churches and cathedrals until oceanic feelings--or possibly anxiety attacks--overcame me, and then I would flee. One day in St. Paul's Cathedral in London, getting ready to flee the vast, vertiginous hall, I grabbed a free brochure, a little green booklet that caught my eye. I took it, went to the tube, caught a train, and started reading this strange pamphlet, titled *A Biologist Looks at Life.* My heart was pounding, as if I were on the verge of a new scientific discovery, and I read the first sentence, "Nobody knows why we sleep." "Ah," I thought at the time, a thought that still comforts me, "if nobody knows why we sleep, I don't need to know why I'm here." Calm washed over me, and instead of feeling all alone, I sensed that the biologist, and indeed all humanity, and I had one great thing in common, we didn't know why we sleep. I could live with not knowing such things as what I was supposed to be doing with myself there in London, if I could live with not knowing the great things--about sleep, about life, about who we were supposed to become, about death.

Sometimes only acceptance will make us whole. Even when every part of ourselves is searching, what we most need to find is the power to stop. Some of the most significant events in life--think of that Chinese fable about the predatory chain that is broken by a random but life-saving stumble--some of the most significant events are random, or have nothing to do with our will, our plans, or our nature. Nobody knows why we sleep. What is interesting to me about that story now is that E.O. Wilson thinks he does know why we sleep, and that doesn't change the point at all. The frontier has pushed back in the last thirty years, and yet there are still things nobody knows; and we won't know even as we learn new answers all the time. Even this is something we can accept. We accept, for if we have searched as sincerely and honestly as we can, our reward will be our knowing that we do not need to know everything yet. We can stop, and let go, accept, and be whole. Why that is, nobody knows. But somehow it seems to be all right.

Resources used to prepare this sermon include Spaulding Gray, *Swimming to Cambodia* (New York: Theater Communications Group, 1985); and Edward O. Wilson, *Consilience: The Unity of Knowledge* (New York: Alfred A. Knopf, 1998).

LET US BE MALADJUSTED

January 16, 2005

In the popular iconic image of Martin Luther King, Jr., we see a man immersed in the practice of nonviolence and the struggle for freedom, but without any of the internal conflicts that accompany such a demanding vocation. He is confident and clear, never doubtful or confused. He is not anxious about the future. His courage never seems to waver. But this image doesn't tell us how he got to be like that. Rather it shows us the legacy of a man who spoke the truth and made it sound simple--although of course, no one knew better than he did that it would never be easy.

King gave us a vision of a world in which "all of God's children... will be able to join hands." He gave us a vision of a future, when "we will be able to emerge... into the bright and glittering daybreak of freedom and justice." His vision is persuasive, clear, and direct in its moral authority. But that vision is grounded in an experience that is neither simple, nor easy: on the contrary, it is profoundly uncomfortable. To use King's word, it is "maladjusted."

When it came time to plan the message for this morning, King's famous line, "Let us be maladjusted," came back to me. It's a phrase that seems to ring with new and relevant truth this year. Perhaps that's because I'm not all that comfortable in our world right now. I wonder what good can come of feeling maladjusted. So I decided to look at what King had to say about it.

King delivered these lines on graduation day at Lincoln University, a historically black college in suburban Pennsylvania. When he says "us," he meant the young African American men and women who were about to enter a world in which they were not very comfortable either. The Civil Rights Act of 1964 was still three turbulent years away. They were all participants in a struggle for justice that had not yet been achieved. When King says "Let us be maladjusted," he is reassuring his listeners that their feelings are legitimate: he shares them.

It's a revealing glimpse of King, who always seemed to be so confident in himself and so clear about his message. For that confidence and that clarity came from someone who was tensely familiar with the discomfort of living in a world that did not treat him fairly. He wasn't thinking only of himself and other African Americans, however. His sense of community was nothing less than global. In his commencement speech he addresses not only racism and its attendant economic injustices, but also militarism and its use of technology for destruction. In a world gone so wrong, any sane and humane person would have to be maladjusted.

"It may well be," King declares, "that the salvation of our world lies in the hands of the maladjusted." The maladjusted have a vision of justice, like Amos; a vision of freedom, like Abraham Lincoln; and a vision of love, like Jesus. Maladjustment is the beginning of social change. That is how it began in Martin Luther King, Jr., and that is how it begins in all of us.

Listen to how "Martin's big words" are used in the children's story we heard earlier. Where a sign says "whites only," Martin remembers that his mother told him, "You are as good as anyone." When he grows up, he studies the teachings of Mahatma Gandhi. "Martin said 'love' when others said 'hate,'" the story goes. "He said 'together,' when others said 'separate.' He said 'peace' when others said 'war.'" When he was told to stop marching, he said 'no.'"

Every step of the way, Martin Luther King refused to do what he was told to do. He may have practiced nonviolence. But he was also oppositional and resistant and not afraid to be the one to say just what people in power did not want to hear. King's tremendous moral authority came from many sources. It came from his belief in equality and his ability to express the truth in a way that people could hear-- sometime for the first time. It came from his willingness to put himself on the line for what was right. It came from his religious faith. And it came from his maladjustment, from his experience of living at odds with the world as it was, and from his refusal to accept it as it was. Maladjustment is a creative tension between what is and what should be. It is a righteous irritant and a developmental boost. It puts us in the uncomfortable gap between where we have been and where we are going. And it is the discomfort we feel there, in that gap, that helps us to grow and change.

Martin Luther King knew that maladjustment was a powerful tool. When he exhorted the Lincoln University graduating class, "Let us be maladjusted," he was asking each and every one of them to join a movement for peace and freedom. He was pointing out the excruciating moral dissonance to be found everywhere--in the larger world and in their world, in India and in Alabama. Out of that dissonance would emerge a vision--"the bright and glittering daybreak of freedom and justice."

These days dissonance surrounds us once again. If we are feeling uncomfortable, perhaps that is a good sign. It could be the beginning of a creative process that will yield a new vision and a renewed sense of hope.

Recent expressions of maladjustment suggest some possibilities. Here's one: Dante Zappala, a part-time teacher, wrote in the *Los Angeles Times* this Friday about the death of his brother. He was killed in Iraq last April. Zappala describes how difficult it has been to explain his brother's death to his nine-year-old son. The announcement this week that no weapons of mass destruction existed in Iraq when our military invaded there nearly two years ago "resonates with profound depth" in his family. Zappala writes, "I have moved from frustration to disappointment to anger. And now I have arrived at a place not of understanding but of hope--blind hope that this will change."

It is hard enough to grieve a brother's death. But when that death cannot even be explained--when the dissonance between what we were told and what is true is finally exposed, the pain is nearly unbearable. The only thing to do is to call for justice. "Let us begin to right the wrongs," Dante Zappala concludes. "Let us be maladjusted," declares Martin Luther King.

In those words we hear his pain and his resistance, his discomfort with the world as it is. In those words we also hear the invitation to use that discomfort to bring about profound social change. Maladjustment is the starting point of transformation.

Let us be maladjusted. Let us take our inspiration from our great leader, Martin Luther King, to move from dissonance and pain to justice and hope. He taught us how: now it is we who shall overcome.

Resources used to prepare this sermon include Martin Luther King, Jr., "The American Dream" in *Testament of Hope: The Essential Writings and Speeches of Martin Luther King, Jr.,* ed. James M. Washington (San Francisco: Harper, 1991); Doreen Rappaport, *Martin's Big Words* (New York: Hyperion Books, 2001); and Dante Zappala, "It's Official: My Brother Died in Vain" in the *Los Angeles Times,* Friday, January 14, 2005.

WALKING THE DOG

SPIRIT OF LIFE: IN EVERY DAY

January 5, 1997

A couple of months ago, I received an invitation from a colleague to contribute to a book he was editing on spirituality in everyday life. Don't take this to mean that someone thinks I am an authority on the subject. I'm sure that he sent the invitation to a hundred of his closest acquaintances, and that he had nothing specifically in mind when he wrote to me. The letter indicated that some of the contributors would be writing on the spirituality of gardening, parenting, meditating, and witnessing for social justice. Presumably I would be able to offer some comparable activity.

So I thought about it for a while. I reviewed a typical day in my life. I wake up; my first thought is something like, "Oh, God, I'm going to die. What does it mean to be alive?" My next thought is, "I'd really like a cup of coffee." Later in the morning, I drive over to the gym. There I pursue one of my most serious spiritual practices, working out. Actually I do meditate on the rowing machine, *in a way*. Where the day takes me from there can vary considerably. Ramping up the freeway I pray, "God, please don't let me die today." Then I turn up the car stereo real loud and meditate, *in a way*. At work, at my desk at home or in the office here, I get serious and think about you. Except when I'm hungry; then I think about food.

But then, food is spiritual if you're really hungry, isn't it? At the end of the day, I come home and play the piano for a while. When I play the piano, I meditate, *in a way*. If it sounds good, it's a spiritual experience. If it sounds bad, it isn't. That's about it. Not too much that I'd want to write for that book, unless I'm willing to say, as I'm obviously tempted to do, that everything I do is spiritual. But then I'd be lying!

When I first planned how I would approach the subject for today, I had in mind that I would show how almost everything in life *can* be spiritual. Sleeping, waking, eating, driving, working, playing-- all the things we do are spiritual. And they are, *in a way*. There's only one problem with that notion. If you look a little more carefully at what you do, you see, as I did, that it is easy to call almost any activity spiritual, and it is also self-serving. The temptation is to justify whatever we do, by saying that it has spiritual value. But if everything is spiritual, then we already have what we need and we don't need to search for understanding or direction. Obviously, that's not how it is for any of us.

Most people come to religious communities like this one searching for something more than they have found in life so far. That search is for something of value and depth, something worthy of a commitment, something ultimate and compelling, that goes beyond everyday life and the self-interest that drives it. There is a glimmering of what we seek in the awareness of our mortality, or in the enjoyment of music or beauty, or in the contemplative quality of some of our tasks, but it's only a glimmering, not a definition or a discipline or a path to follow. For that, we turn to a community like this one.

Our work is to help each other find definition, discipline, and a path to follow in the search for a meaningful spiritual life. What we have to offer must show some honesty, some rigor, and some reason. If it does not, then we are as lazy and deluded as Peter Marin claims any of us can be: knocking off a designer god who meets every one of our needs and justifies our self-absorption.

What is spirituality, if it can be defined at all? It is what many of you say you have come here seeking: something of value and depth, something sustaining, something worthy of commitment. Spirituality teaches us to understand and experience life in terms of ultimate reality. As Parker J. Palmer defined it, spirituality is "an effort to penetrate the illusions of the external world and to name its underlying truth." Spirituality is about reality, not illusion, and if we want to practice it with integrity, we must concern ourselves with the difference at all times. The difference is not always what we think.

In A. A. Milne's disarming little poem, Elizabeth Ann goes to find how God began. When her nurse won't tell her, she searches for an "Important Man." But he cannot tell her either. So Elizabeth Ann comes home and asks her doll Jennifer Jane to tell her where God began. And Jennifer Jane tells her, in words only Elizabeth Ann can understand. But evidently she speaks the truth. "O! thank you, Jennifer," she says. "Now I know." Ultimate reality is not about the world as it appears on the surface. Ultimate reality is the truth that penetrates and underlies the external world. Lord High Doodelum and his coachman may have power, but a doll named Jennifer Jane knows the truth.

If truth about ultimate reality can come from a doll, perhaps it can come from anywhere. When is our spirituality the real thing, and when is it just another scam, as Peter Marin would have it, perpetrated on us by any number of "gurus, sages, charismatic poseurs, preachers, therapists, and snake-oil salesmen?" Our spiritual search can take us from one place to another, adopting one direction, then another, committing finally to nothing, coming up empty.

The risk of undertaking any kind of spiritual pursuit is great, if you rely on someone else to tell you what it is. No one can tell you what ultimate reality is. A teacher can show you how to see it, perhaps, or a spiritual practice can guide you to where it is inside you, or an important event can strip away your illusions and show you truth--but you must decide what is real or what is phony, what is worthy of your commitment or needing to be discarded. You get to judge reality for yourself. And next, you must judge yourself as well.

From time to time I have taken meditation training. Each time I have the same powerful experience. As I enter meditation, I become aware that there is what I can only describe as a parallel frequency or band-width, a reality that hums along just below the surface of my usual thoughts. I can go there in meditation. I feel as if I am stepping into the river of the infinite flow, beyond time or space, and that it is inside me. It's a wonderful experience. I believe that it contains some truth that would help me, somehow, if I could only maintain the discipline of going there more often.

I'd like to tell you that this is my spirituality. It could be. But the truth is, I only do it when someone is telling me to. My yearning for ultimate reality, for the river of the infinite flow beyond time and space is not strong enough, evidently. Those occasional excursions to it, however, have given me a sense of what makes something spiritual for me. I have the feeling that there is truth in what I have experienced, and that other things I do, tasks that are meditative and pull me in that direction, are spiritual for that reason.

But I need to stay honest about it. I'm not always meditating when I'm on the rowing machine. Sometimes I'm churning out one self-interested little fantasy after another; or making a list; or watching the calorie-counter display and figuring out what I can eat later on. I can't say that rowing is spiritual. But sometimes, when I set myself into motion, and my meditative mind goes to that river of infinite flow, something spiritual is happening to me. I cannot tell you if I am a better person because it does. But I can tell you I am a better person when I admit to myself it only happens some of the time.

Whatever we do may be spiritual if it takes us in the direction of ultimate reality, if it points to an awareness that underlies the preoccupations of the external world and all its delusions. That is why you may comfortably claim any activity, even an unlikely one, as your spiritual work. There is probably something every one of us does that opens up somehow to contemplate ultimate reality; whatever that is could be our spiritual direction.

But simply naming it is not enough. And that is why it takes some rigor and some honesty to practice spirituality. It's work. It has standards, although they are not the usual standards. And it makes us grow if we practice it well. If gardening or running or meditating serve as your spiritual work, then use these practices to take you beyond the immediate benefits they might offer. It's good to make the yard look nice or to reduce stress or your heart rate, but these activities can really work for you if you let them help you see reality in an altered way. Running is more than staying fit; it's experiencing the joy of being in a physical body, of being aware, by an immediate and arduous effort, that you are alive. Be open to the ideas and thoughts that come to you as you go; as anxiety and stress dissolve in the flood of endorphins, ask yourself what really matters most to you. You may find the answers to be--quite spiritual. You may tell yourself that you are part of something larger than your lone jogging self; that you--whoever you are and however unlikely that might be--are fulfilling your role in some larger purpose, one you may not know but sense anyway.

These are just words. But I say them to give to you my own sense of the ordinariness, the personal and idiosyncratic nature of spiritual experience, and I say them to give to you what I believe is its legitimacy. If it's truly yours, you can trust it. If you ask it to teach you, to go beneath the surface of the external world, to the realm of ultimate reality, you may find yourself sustained and held by something that becomes more real to you every day.

If there is one thing I know, at least for myself, it is that something becomes more real the more I search and sense what seems ultimate, deep, and sustaining. If you come here for no other reason than to hear others tell you that the search really does matter and that what you find for yourself you can trust if it's yours, then I would say you have found something precious. Keep it. Talk about it if you can find the words and don't mind sounding just slightly ridiculous. Or leave that job to me. But keep looking, for what you may hope to find is somewhere very close to you indeed.

Resources used to prepare this sermon include Peter Marin, "An American Yearning," *Harper's Magazine* (1996): 35-43; A.A. Milne, "Explained" in *Now We Are Six* (New York: E.P. Dutton & Co., Inc., 1927); and Parker J. Palmer, "Leading From Within" (Wellesley College, 2005). Lecture available from the worldwide web <http://forum.wgbh.org/wgbh/forum.php?lecture_id=2047>.

WALKING THE DOG

December 30, 2001

This summer--which now seems like a simpler time, already belonging to a distant past--I didn't do much. I made several trips to New Jersey to see my parents. My father's health was declining; we arranged hospice care and waited for the end. In between visits I was unable to concentrate on my usual summer projects; even reading was difficult. Anticipatory grief put everything on hold. Vacations were considered, then postponed. Time passed.

Eventually I realized that it is not possible to be productive and sad at the same time. So I let my distracted state of mind claim its season of my life. One ritual gave me solace, a thing to do at regular intervals, a task that took increasingly greater amounts of time: walking Aki, our young dog. We walked for miles every day, to the park and the college campus. We did all our errands on foot. I timed our excursions to maintain Aki's burgeoning dog social life, so that he would not miss the encounters with Cleo, Brownie, Buddy, Owen, and Coco, that are the highlight of his day.

In my neighborhood I became a familiar local character. Driven by one clear purpose--to socialize my dog--I approached strangers, talked to them, learned who lived on my street. After years of coming and going from my home by way of a garage on an alley, I was seeing where I lived for the first time. This simple activity, walking the dog, became a comfort and a refuge. As the summer went by, I began to notice how many ways it helped me and kept me whole.

Now that the year has come and gone and brought its distracted sadness upon us all, those hours outside with Aki are more essential than ever. I tell you about them because each of us needs something--a simple ritual, a way to calm ourselves, and a community around us, to survive all the hard times in life. These days we live under a cloud of uncertainty. Yearning to return to normalcy, but finding it impossible to do so, feeling the waves of impact hit us so close to home--as jobs turn shaky, investments shrivel, and security evaporates--our simple rituals are all we can count on for comfort and refuge. Our rituals are not frivolous. They are life itself. And they help us remember what it means to be at peace.

Mark Taylor, a professor of religion at Williams College in Massachusetts, offered a perspective in the *Los Angeles Times* recently on how the terrorist attack has changed the American psyche. "Individually and collectively," he wrote, "we sense the danger of things slipping out of control and are not sure how or where to respond." He argued that we should not seek to find closure too soon. Rather, we should let the anxiety we carry and the wounds we have sustained teach us their spiritual lessons. We must "humbly accept our vulnerability by opening ourselves to help from others ...without whom we cannot survive."

We have been through a life-altering ordeal, our losses mount, we are not the same. "I wish the World Trade Center did not fall down," said one child, during services at our church, after it happened. So do we all. We are still struggling with that basic fact.

You can't think about *it* all the time. Even if you are learning something from your anxiety, you need to find safety, respite and comfort somewhere. My need intensified with each passing day of my father's slow decline and the quickening crisis in our world. I savor those moments when I'm not thinking about *it*. *It* is far too big for me to handle.

Time has passed. My father has died, and our nation has gone to war. Some things are settled, but much is not. Anxiety is still a familiar state of mind. We are going places again, but we keep looking over our shoulder, suspicious of strangers. I still talk to them when I'm walking my dog.

At 6:30 in the morning it is just growing light outside, and I haven't had my coffee yet. Dog walkers speak without introductions or coffee, however. One I've never met before approaches Aki and me. "Was your dog the star of 'Best in Show'?" he asks.

I smile over this question for days. Only in Los Angeles, where I have never been mistaken for a movie star, does someone think my dog is. But I am grateful for friendliness and for strangers who want to meet my dog. I am glad for moments in time when inane conversation is a respite from the hard, heavy news we must hear all day long.

The walks are more than an escape, however. They connect me

to other people. When I am grieving or feeling vulnerable, it is easy to feel alone and disconnected. Though I am reserved, my dog is not--and he has brought me into contact with people I never would have met any other way. I've talked to security guards at Santa Monica College, homeless people recycling in the alley, nannies strolling children in the park, kids on skateboards after school. In the months I have been walking my dog, I have met so many new people that every house on my street between our home and the park shelters some person or pet I now know. I live in a different place because of our walks. And it's a better place because I know it.

One of the lessons I've received from the simple act of walking my dog is how knowing a place makes it better. Until I walked up and down our street at all hours of day and night, I felt no attachment to my neighborhood. My allegiance was only as great as the cluster of five townhouses that makes up our homeowners' association. We're a friendly little group, but I have a real neighborhood now. There is safety and comfort in knowing your neighborhood.

Mark Taylor wrote in his essay in the *Los Angeles Times*, we cannot survive unless we open ourselves to others, "both within and beyond the borders that we now know are insecure." This is a global as well as local truth. We need to know our neighbors--and not just the ones next door, or in the next state.

All the world's peoples are our neighbors now. If we know each other, we make the world a better and a safer place. That is what peace looks like to me these days. Walking the dog has also given me a sense of inner peace. When I'm not talking to the neighbors, I turn contemplative. Our pace is slow, like a walking meditation, as Aki sniffs every inch of turf in his ever-expanding universe. There is nothing else to do but turn inward. I have never returned from a walk without feeling different in some way, even when nothing at all has happened. Slowing down and attending to the rhythms of a dog are one way to deal with anxiety. It's as if the things that worry me go away for a while. When they come back, they have become less worrisome or found a solution. Sometimes they do not come back at all.

I live near Santa Monica airport. The sound of the planes, once a minor nuisance, now gets my attention in a different way and makes me uneasy. Out walking, the noise is loud sometimes. There may be no running away from what makes me anxious, but I can keep walking. That thought calms me. I think there is such a thing as inner peace. It tells me to keep walking.

In the time ahead, we will need to live with our anxiety and our wounds, and to learn the lessons they have to teach. We have no choice but to meet challenges that may alter our way of life. We will look deeply into the values and assumptions of the American dream and struggle with what it means now. We have sober and difficult tasks ahead.

But none of us will be able to do our part unless we keep the rituals that calm us inside and connect us to our world. Whatever your rituals may be: making dinner at home with your family, entering and sitting in this space before the service, writing in your journal or emailing your friends, whatever you do that is simple, calming and affirming of life, keep doing it. Let your acts of custom and connection give you the strength for the time ahead. Center yourself in the rituals of your days. Remember that peace can be as ordinary and common as the simple things people do, wherever we live, in a world where neighbors meet.

Resources used to prepare this sermon include Mark C. Taylor, "Terror, Anxiety and Awe are on the Loose at Ground Zero," *Los Angeles Times*, Friday, September 28, 2001.

OUR FATHER

June 17, 2001

The Algonquin Indian Big Thunder divided up his world into two realities, both essential, but different from each other. The Great Spirit is our father: "In all things, the air we breathe," he wrote, but "the earth is our mother." Of all the images of father in the sacred texts of the world, I like this one best.

As long as I have been a minister, the image of God the father has had scant acceptance among religious liberals. I went to divinity school when the feminist critique of patriarchal religion was at its most imaginative, angry and insistent. Mary Daly's ground-breaking, influential work, *Beyond God the Father*, was published just before I became a theological student. Daly was a former Catholic scholar who knew patriarchal religion from the inside, having studied at the Vatican. When she railed against the Church, she had the goods. Daly's thesis was based in the insight that if God is father, then men are gods--just look at the way our society is organized. Everything from domestic violence to our economic system is rooted in this wild imbalance of power. I still think she has a point.

The quest for balance has put father out of action in recent years. Some have sought explicitly female images of the divine, and the search has uncovered important ancient history and empowered a new generation of women with spiritual practices to use for self-knowledge and healing. Others have simply dropped the gender out of divinity altogether.

I could say more, but something holds me back. As I prepared for this Father's Day Sunday, and the trip to Cleveland this week for the Unitarian Universalist General Assembly, I have also been arranging a trip to New Jersey, where my parents live, and the meeting I will have with the hospice agency about the care of my dying father. So my mind keeps wandering to the specifics of my father's life--and imminent death, and the impact he has had on me, and on what this has to do with these spiritual images and issues I have studied. The personal, as we feminists have often observed, is the political, and the boundary between the two is neither crisp nor clear.

May Sarton--a Unitarian Universalist, to whose work I frequently turn in search of the right words for a memorial service-- wrote a poem titled "My Father's Death":

> I shall not be a daughter anymore,
> But through this final parting, all stripped down,
> Launched on the tide of love, go out full grown.

Losing a father is a rite of passage, as daughters and sons give up not only their fathers but their role as children. We give up seeing ourselves as the object of the parental gaze, approving or disapproving; we are no longer a reflection.

When anyone we love dies, our Unitarian Universalist philosophy teaches us, the one we love lives on inside us, becomes part of us. And as we know ourselves, "full grown," as May Sarton puts it, we see what parts we carry on from those who have gone before.

The closer we come to my father's death, the closer I look at his life, and mine, and see how much his spirit is still the air I breathe.

My father's formal education had a late start, as he spent the first couple years of college at Juilliard Conservatory, studying music. In his family, music was God. But he realized that the cornet was not his vocation, and eventually decided to go to college.

At the University of Chicago, where my father studied English, one teacher, Norman MacLean, shaped his intellectual imagination. MacLean later became quite well known as the author of stories about his early years in Montana: one book, *A River Runs Through It*, even became a feature film. At my father's fiftieth Chicago reunion, he sought out MacLean--also an old man by then, and told him what an influence he had been. It was an uncharacteristically sentimental gesture for my father.

My father went to graduate school in English at Harvard. When the war broke out, he enlisted in the Army. One of our favorite family stories is that my father, filling out his enlistment form, wrote in the tiny space allotted for his academic background, "ENG" for "English," but which the Army assumed meant "Engineering." They sent him to radar school.

The war years brought marriage to my mother, my older brother Richard, overseas assignments in Japan and the Philippines, and eventually, employment. Because of his long academic sojourn, comfortable financial background, and the war, my father did not hold a job until he was in his mid-thirties! When he did go to work, he joined the wave of post-war corporate workers, settled down at RCA, and never left. I note that he hired RCA's first African-American engineer.

Always a liberal, principled and progressive, but too quiet for his own good, my father is not a religious man. Raised in a non-observant Jewish home, when he married my mother, a Protestant, they resolved the problem of what to do with the children by joining a Unitarian Universalist church. There my father and mother became active members. But his core philosophy still reached back to his Chicago days, and the golden era when he was educated in the "great books" and classical tradition of--dare I say it--patriarchal thought. He named my younger brother after Geoffrey Chaucer. We were requested to recite long memorized passages from Homer at the dinner table.

I learned to play the piano, and showed some signs of following in his path to conservatory. But music became too emotionally fraught for me. I could never sit down to play without my father suggesting how to improve some incredibly minor bit of phrasing, until I nearly refused to play in his presence at all.

He was a ruthless editor of my writing too. Just a couple of months ago, after reading a sermon I delivered here, his only comment was, "I found some typos." Still, he took pride and interest in my work, and Unitarian Universalism has been a strong bond between me and both my parents.

I know that the parts of myself that are self-critical, that struggle to perform up to ridiculously high standards, that withhold for fear of not being good enough, result from the influence my father had on me. No child can grow up without certain emotional wounds, and those are mine. But I also know that my love of music and writing, and the good strong liberal values I learned from watching him, counterbalance those deficits. My father spoke to me about his philosophy and principles. He encouraged me to think for myself and tell him what was on my mind. Because of him, I enjoy the company of men and have never stopped learning. May Sarton writes,

> Alone now in my life, no longer child,
> This hour and its flood of mystery
> Where death and love are reconciled,
> Launches the ship of my history.

It's a compact and beautiful way of speaking about how we become who we are, and how grief is the nexus of growth. Her words also suggest how *our* words for the divine--whether they be God the father, the mother, or a de-genderized image that makes no distinctions, have meaning only if they connect us to these life experiences: to the love, the loss, and even the wounds by which we grow.

The air we breathe, Big Thunder said, is the Great Spirit, our father. And the earth is our mother. Some of us may be inclined more strongly towards one or the other. Some of us had a mother or a father but not one of each, for loving parents of either gender--alone or in partnership, can make a good home for children. Some of us have adults in our lives who have been parents to us, even though we were not related by biological connection or by kinship.

But we all still need the air we breathe and the earth that holds us close. We all still need the father and mother elements of the universe that balance and draw out the life energy within us. Whatever image of the divine we may choose to give to this relationship, it is the one that gives us life, teaches us to grow, and someday leaves us to be on our own.

During these sad times, I remember that the air I breathe is all around me. I cannot separate myself from it, nor live without it; the Great Spirit, our father, is in this air and in all things, past and present, and yes, even in the days ahead.

Resources used to prepare this sermon include Mary Daly, *Beyond God the Father: Toward a Philosophy of Women's Liberation* (Boston: Beacon Press, 1985); and May Sarton, "My Father's Death" in *May Sarton: Collected Poems 1930-1993* (New York and London: W.W. Norton & Company, 1993).

YOUR SPIRITUAL LIFE

May 8, 1994

Perhaps I learned it from my mother, who always made it clear that we children came into the world because our parents wanted us-- although, she affirmed this rather obliquely at times, declaring that children don't ask to be born, a metaphysical problem I began pondering at a very early age, thanks to her. She taught me that parenthood is a choice we make, one way or the other, and that choice says more about who *we* are than about what our children may owe us.

No two people, or mothers, are alike in this sense, and how we actually feel on occasions such as Mother's Day may differ greatly from each other. Public sentiments on family holidays disguise the fact that our private reflection may be seething with regret or resentment, or lingering over contentment and satisfaction, or vacillating with ambivalence; whatever it is, the words on the card don't quite capture it.

I know my mother well, but I don't know what her reflections today will tell her about the choices she has made. Her inner life and its inner reckonings may have very little to do with me. For her life and her choices are hers all alone. And so are yours. For no matter how actively related you may be to your own family or friends, you are the one whose life you are living, and your determinations and inclinations tell your story and no one else's.

It is in this sense that I speak today of your spiritual life. It is the story--made of dreams and decisions, struggle and survival, of the person you have become. You may not be what you consider to be a spiritual person: you don't pray, you don't know much about religion, you don't even know if you belong in church, but none of that tells the story of your spiritual life. Your spiritual life is whatever life *you* live, and your insight and imagination can teach you the rest. The poet Mary Oliver wrote,

> The path to heaven
> doesn't lie down in flat miles.

It's in the imagination
with which you perceive
this world,
and the gestures
with which you honor it.

Like the conventions surrounding Mother's Day, conventions about the path to heaven may or may not have anything to do with you. There may be archetypal elements--found in dreams, myths, and symbols--that all people share, but these elements do not show the same way to everyone.

One of the great insights Unitarian Universalism reveals to those who come our way is that whatever you have come to understand, however idiosyncratic, about the meaning of your life, there is the center of your spirituality. You may possess insight and wisdom that even you did not recognize as spiritual depth, but it may be exactly that. In your imagination and in your gestures there is all you need to find your way, if you trust yourself and the truth you can discover.

Many years ago, shortly before I went to divinity school, I had a dream that took me years to understand. This dream now recurs from time to time, and when it does, I know what message I am supposed to receive. I dream about a house in which I once lived, a large, antique colonial house with a front and back staircase connected by a long hallway upstairs, and a couple of rooms downstairs added on later to what was once the woodshed. The first time I dreamed the dream, I still lived there. In the dream, I walk down the upstairs hallway, and continue beyond the point where the house actually ends, until I reach a secret, undiscovered wing. This wing has beautiful old rooms, just like the rest of the house, full of colorful quilts and rocking chairs, and I am amazed to find them in this place, which I thought I knew so well.

When I awakened from the dream the first time, I felt happy and energized, as if my own personal universe had expanded, much to my pleasure. I have to admit, some of that expansiveness arose from the dream's illusion that all these rooms and furnishings actually were mine, as if I presided over some colonial manor, but mostly what I felt was the sense of discovery of something that had been there all along, hidden and powerful. This dream has since become my image for my own spiritual life, as if the house were myself, the secret wing, something new for me to explore, something comfortable, inviting, and beautiful.

The first time I had this dream I couldn't help but wonder, when I awakened, where was the rest of this house. It was where I lived, and the dream was so realistic, that my own home acquired the surreal, superadded quality of an unseen presence. I have since lived in many different houses, but when I dream the dream, I go back to that house, and it is as inviting and comfortable as it always was. Through this dream my imagination gave form and shape to the idea that there is a part of myself that I can visit, to explore my spirit and its truth. Now that I know that, I don't hesitate to open the door.

I recently read an interview with writer Jane Hirshfield, who has edited an anthology of poetry called *Women in Praise of the Sacred*. The interviewer commented that the anthology celebrates "the certainty of change, the inevitability of paradox, the ageless marriage of passion and wisdom, and [the poets'] unquenchable desire to sing about their lives." That is what the literature of spirituality encompasses, but Jane Hirshfield's comment is more succinct: "I was reminded that the path is always *a path*," she said. "There is this old simplistic idea that something goes bang and you are enlightened forever. Collecting these poems has taught me it's not so." And so it is for all of us: we can study the texts, practice the disciplines, and read the dreams, but the path is still always a path. Your spiritual life is what your days yield, one after the other, and become the story of who you are.

If you are a woman, Mother's Day is one of those times when you become more intensely aware of whether your days have yielded offspring, and if they have, what has become of them--and you--ever since. Whatever combination of biology and intentionality brought you to that relation may teach you something about your spiritual life as well. If you have children, then you know what transformations in yourself have been brought about by the responsibility and love you hold for another being. If you do not have children, then perhaps you have learned, as I have, that life imposes its own limits on each of us in different ways, and that each of us must accept in terms specific and personal that we may not know everything, do everything, or be everything we hoped. Out of these realities grows our spiritual life too.

In this kind of development, through myriad choices, some carefully wrought, others achieved only by default, we struggle and move along on the spiritual path. Jane Hirshfield writes, "The world asks of us only the strength we have and we give it. Then it asks more, and we give it." The suffering and struggles that accompany us through life give us many opportunities to wonder whether we have the strength, or the endurance, to give what we are asked to give. And as we all know, so much suffering and struggle seems wasteful, so pointless; it only uses people up, it doesn't help them to grow. And that is true. But it is still part of who we are as spiritual beings. And for some mysterious reason we are not diminished by this fact.

One hope I take from my own struggles is that I can never know what purpose they serve while they afflict me. Some of the worst misery I have experienced has later produced some of the most sustaining insights, revelations actually, which have made me who I am in ways that I am proud to claim. I don't know why that is. But my spiritual life and yours do not consist of one elegant finesse after another, of that I am certain. Wisdom arises out of wretchedness as well as abundance; nothing is neat and tidy.

Jane Hirshfield comments, "You can't become wise without giving up some idea of purity that stands in the way of full knowledge." She points to mythological figures such as Pandora and Prometheus, whose mischief and trickery brought wisdom *and* misery into the world, archetypal examples of bad behavior giving rise to enlightenment. Your bad behavior may do that too. Even though it's not what your mother told you. We grow from more than one way of being in the world, and not all of them are safe and predictable.

But the path leads to wisdom, if we give ourselves the time and the stillness to see where we are going. And that is not always easy for people like us. Unitarian Universalists are people of the word: the search for truth, which is the dynamic affirmation of our faith, is conducted almost entirely in reading, writing, talking, debating: speech, not silence, is our custom. And not just any kind of speech: speech with footnotes is the best kind of all. At our best, we practice an intellectual rigor that breaks through conventional thought with originality and energy. At our worst, we are pedants. As important as discourse may be, the spirit moves through more than one medium; speech is one, but silence is another.

"I don't know exactly what a prayer is," Mary Oliver wrote, "I do know how to pay attention, how to fall down into the grass, how to kneel down in the grass, how to be idle and blessed." Her instinct moves her to do just what the spirit needs to come to life: to pay attention, to be still in the grass, to be idle and wordless. We don't need to know what prayer is if we can do that. When you sit still, when you meditate, or do whatever it is that you are called to in silence, you can feel, without words, the flow of infinity that runs through you and around you; that is indeed the whole of being, to which you belong, and where you may rest at the end of your words and restore your soul. Your spiritual life needs silence too.

"The path to heaven doesn't lie down in flat miles. It's in the imagination with which you perceive this world, and the gestures with which you honor it," Mary Oliver wrote, and the imagination and the gestures are our dreams and struggles and silence that yield wisdom to those who wait for it. That wisdom is simply this: "Wild and precious life," as Mary Oliver called it, is everything--and the only thing--that matters; not simply our own lives, solitary and self-determined, but the life we are given and the self we give to it in the end. All dreams, struggles, and silence lead us there, where there is beauty and peace, a home for the spirit; and we are always almost there.

Resources used to prepare this sermon include Jane Hirshfield, ed., *Women in Praise of the Sacred* (New York: Harper Perennial, 1995); and Mary Oliver, "The Swan" and "Summer Day" in *House of Light* (Boston: Beacon Press, 1990).

LIFE IS AN ODYSSEY

March 28, 2004

From time to time, at gatherings of Unitarian Universalist ministers, a senior minister presents the odyssey. The odyssey is a spiritual autobiography. It is the story of how we came to ministry, and where our calling has taken us, internally and externally, over the years. This April, I will be the one to present my odyssey to my colleagues. I am already contemplating what to say and wondering what I will learn from the exercise. I notice that I have already told much of my story, in installments, over the years, in sermons. "I was always an anxious child," I might start off; or, "I come from an interfaith Jewish Christian family, and my parents decided to join the Unitarian Universalist church." Whatever I say, it will be selective. But it will also be true. Somehow I will compose a story of my life.

The Odyssey is also an epic poem. It tells the story of Odysseus, hero of ancient Greece, whose struggles were far more arduous than those of any minister. He spent ten years fighting in Troy and another ten years trying to get home to his family. In all that time, his wife Penelope and son Telemachos knew nothing about what had happened to him. Penelope spent her life fending off unwanted suitors. Telemachos grew up, became a man, and set off on his own journey to search for his father.

In the years of wanderings and adventures, Odysseus overcame many obstacles, natural and supernatural. Up above, the gods manipulated and interfered with all his efforts. When he finally arrived home, even his reunion with his wife and the requisite annihilation of her suitors was orchestrated by Athene, militant goddess of wisdom.

I couldn't help but think about *The Odyssey* when I accepted my assignment to speak to the ministers. For *The Odyssey* is a work of the imagination, not a recounting of facts. And the stories it tells convinces the reader that the gods, not the humans, call the shots. Odysseus is a brave man but he is also a pawn of the real players, as Zeus and Athene act out their own drama through him. If life is an odyssey, we have even less to say about it than we think we do.

The Odyssey of Homer and the contemporary spiritual biography, however, share much in common. They tell of struggles and triumphs. They don't pass over the wanderings, which may at first have seemed pointless, but took us where we needed to go. And we who tell these stories hear the larger meanings emerge; they instruct us and make us whole. "Deep down in some long-encumbered self," writes Michael Blumenthal, "it is the story you have been writing all your life, where no Calypso holds you against your own willfulness, where you can rise from the bleak island of your old story and tread your way home."

Everyone has a story to tell. Dan Wakefield, author of *The Story of Your Life*, a guide to writing your spiritual autobiography, observed, "No doubt the first humans, sitting around the fires of their caves, told stories relating their life experience to the power and mystery of the universe." And for many people, not just Odysseus, the role of God--or gods--has been central.

Dan Wakefield also mentioned in his book that the Puritans-- our Unitarian spiritual forebears--cultivated the personal testimonial as religious expression. People of faith frequently spoke about the role of God in their lives. Their churches even required such speeches before admitting them into membership. We dropped that requirement a long time ago. But the spiritual autobiography is still a lively part of our faith tradition.

I will soon get my chance to tell my story. Ministers listen carefully to the telling of the odyssey. I can remember when I, much younger, heard this narrative for the first time. The story was compelling, but even more memorable were the respect and the fellow-feeling the group brought to the occasion. It is perhaps the only time in life when a group of people (especially other ministers) will listen for an hour, with rapt attention, to one of their peers.

The same time I accepted the task of composing my odyssey, I began to think about what it would be like for our congregation, if some of you took a turn offering your spiritual autobiography to us. What if, once or twice a year, some of our senior members prepared an odyssey, and a group gathered to listen to the story of that life? It's something I'd like to see us try sometime.

Dan Wakefield noted that this can be a very powerful

experience. You may already have a feeling for the potential in such an exercise. If you are a journal writer, you know the sense of altered reality that comes from recounting your personal history. High school seniors working on college admission essays get a taste of how much can ride and fall on the way we represent ourselves in words. Some of you may be writing memoirs, or assembling family histories for grandchildren. Whatever the purpose, the story of a life is a powerful tool and builder of human connections. Especially in the telling of it.

One of the participants in Dan Wakefield's spiritual autobiography class observed, "What I found is I could write something and read it to myself and it would probably have little impact, but if I'm with someone else and read it aloud, there's something about another person's presence that makes it 'ring true.' It's much more powerful." It's not just the writing of the story, it's being heard by another.

What "rings true" is honesty. Honesty is a relational value. It discloses our true selves, and builds understanding between people. It deepens our bond with others. Telling our story can also heal us. Recent brain research has shown that people recover from trauma when they are able to talk about it. What happens is something more than simply discharging a bad memory. Constructing a narrative of our experience changes the brain and consolidates the recovery.

Speaking our history transforms our past. It becomes a story, with selected events and interpretation. We create a view of ourselves that allows us to understand and forgive our failings and misadventures. Dan Wakefield says, "Since our past experience only exists now in our own mind--it only 'lives' in our recreation of it--our changed experience of it becomes the reality, and in that sense we really do have the power to change our own past."

This transformation is not denial or wiping out of memory. It's not "rewriting history like a totalitarian government which recreates its nation's past to fit the latest political dogma." Rather, through writing and telling, we re-experience our past from the perspective of who we are today. That knowledge and distance give new meaning to who we once were.

"Say you finally invented a new story of your life," writes Michael Blumenthal. "It is not the story of your defeat or of your impotence and powerlessness before the large forces of wind and accident." It is another story, one that tells the truth, and heals the soul, and makes you wise. "It is the story you have been writing all your life."

The new story is also an old story, rooted in the common ground of all humanity. Perhaps this is why it is so important to have someone to listen. For it truly is something we share. Each story is related to every other story. Not just stories from today, but the story of every seeker and wanderer, who, like Odysseus, wants only to find the way home. A larger pattern emerges out of the myriad details and trials of life. It shows us who we are against the backdrop of mystery: heroes, like Odysseus, in a life we can never fully understand. The pattern shows how we prevail, each in our own way, in the purpose of becoming fully ourselves. It is a struggle worthy of an epic poem all our own, one that only we can write.

Resources used to prepare this sermon include *The Odyssey of Homer*, trans. Richmond Lattimore (New York: Harper & Row, 1967); and Dan Wakefield, *The Story of Your Life* (Boston: Beacon Press, 1990).

AN UNEXPECTED BREAK

June 13, 2004

The knuckle that joins my pinky to my left hand is gone forever. In the catalog of potential deformities, a missing knuckle is so negligible it might not even make the list. But it was mine, and I can't help but acknowledge the wrenching irrevocability of its departure.

Five weeks ago, while attending a meeting in Boston, I fell down half a flight of stairs, broke my hand, and dislocated my shoulder. I'd never broken a bone before. When I returned home I asked my doctor what to expect. He said, "Set your psyche. A broken hand is a small injury, but you'll be surprised how disabling it is."

It is a small injury. I did not need surgery, and only spent a month in a cast. And yet, as any of you who have talked to me have no doubt observed, I haven't handled it well. The adjustments needed to accomplish daily tasks in a cast were daunting. My dependency on others was humbling. The story about my accident was not very colorful and garnered little interest. The first week or two I experienced a daily meltdown induced by frustration, pain and unrealistic expectations.

I took a lot of taxis. Each driver had something to say about broken bones. The most memorable driver was one whose mother had broken her hand at the age of seventy-four. "She fell down the stairs and hurt herself because she was trying to save a plate of cookies she had just baked. She was always active, doing things," he said. After the fall, she had to let others wait on her, which was difficult. But then, unfortunately, before her one hand was healed, she took another fall and broke her other one. "She never got out of her chair again," the driver told me. Such cheerful encounters started my workday. By the time I arrived at my office, I was already out of sorts.

The taxi driver's story was a good warning for me. Even a small disability puts you at risk for larger ones. It took time to get used to the heavy weight on my left arm, and as I lurched around, off balance, I realized how easily I could fall again.

This is the state of vulnerability into which I was thrust. Many of you know it well. When I asked, one Sunday morning a while back, how many of you had ever broken a bone, nearly all of you raised your hands. That was a revelation. I had been living in a fool's paradise of invincibility, at least as far as my strong bones could take me. I realized that there was a lot I didn't know--about living with disability, about accepting limitations, about needing help, about growing in compassion.

At some point in this experience, however, I was able to take a step back from feeling sorry for myself. When I did, it began to dawn on me that I had a very small window on the life that many disabled people must lead. Perhaps they too start the day by bracing themselves for the many obstacles they will have to overcome. Perhaps they too dissolve in tears on a regular basis. Perhaps they too wish they didn't have to go through this.

I thought of all the people in this congregation who suffer from disabling conditions, some of them progressive or chronic. I could look forward to a full recovery--minus the knuckle, no big deal. But many of you and the people you love have far greater adjustments to make. I grew in respect for how well each and every one of you copes with the challenges you face. I also realized that sooner or later we each have to face our decline. Even a small disability is a reminder of how contingent our well-being truly is.

The folk singer Fred Small, who is also a Unitarian Universalist minister, has written a funny and provocative song, the "Talking Wheelchair Blues." In it he chronicles how a spunky woman in a wheelchair faces discrimination of all kinds--social, spatial, political. But she is philosophical about it. "I look at it this way," she says. "In fifty years you'll be in worse shape than I am now. See, we're all the same, this human race. Some of us are called disabled. And the rest--well, the rest of you are just temporarily able-bodied."

The human condition will make us all vulnerable and needy some time. However invincible we may imagine ourselves to be, the truth will catch up with us. And then we will be grateful for the compassion others have to give. Nothing is more comforting than the kind words of those who have been through the same ordeal. Those of you who also suffered through broken bones and casts, thank you for telling me about it. You reminded me of what it means to be human.

For what draws us together, it turns out, is what makes us fall apart. The funeral ritual of the past week for former president Ronald Reagan has brought to awareness once again how even the most powerful people can be leveled by disability. Illness democratizes us the way no other experience can.

While I was sitting around with the cast on, I decided to read the memoir by Michael J. Fox, titled *Lucky Man*. Michael J. Fox lives with Parkinson's disease, an incurable degenerative condition. It's a disease with which I am all too familiar, as my father suffered from it for over fifteen years. Several members of our congregation also live with this disability, which tends to set in late in life.

In the case of Michael J. Fox, however, he began to experience symptoms at the age of thirty. Learning to cope with the personal and public aspects of a neurological condition, its symptoms plainly and dramatically visible, proved to be a huge challenge for this successful young actor. His story is well worth reading.

He relates one of the many funny incidents that led him to acceptance. It occurred in 1994, while making a film with Woody Allen. While they were killing time on the set, someone asked, "If you could live in any era other than the present, what would it be?" Woody Allen's answer was, "I wouldn't want to live in any time prior to the invention of penicillin."

"Everybody fell out laughing--it was such a perfect, in-character response. With everything that Woody Allen was going through that spring, there was still nothing more terrifying to him than the prospect of incurable disease. And then suddenly it hit me," Michael J. Fox admits. *"Hey, I have an incurable disease--and I'm laughing anyway. I must be doing okay."*

Today Michael J. Fox heads a non-profit foundation to raise funds to find a cure for Parkinson's. He is a prominent advocate for embryonic stem-cell research. He credits the compassion shown to him by others in the patient community for the work he is now inspired to do. "They've helped me see that my story is not only my story," he concludes. "We *are* a we, in the boat together, and awaiting the same rescue. Don't lose hope, because it's coming."

There is much for any of us to learn, understand, and accept about our human condition. But fundamental to learning any of it is the realization that being human is not about getting to the top of the mountain, as Pema Chödron illustrated so clearly in the reading today. We find our true nature by going down, not up. We cannot transcend suffering, only experience it. "We explore the reality and unpredictability of insecurity and pain," she writes, "and we try not to push it away." We move down into it. "With us move millions of others, our companions in awakening from fear."

What we discover at the bottom is compassion. This is the hard-won gift, the "love that will not die," the bond that makes us one with each other. This is not only what helps us to cope with disability. It is what makes our lives worth living.

Most of the time I had my cast on, I felt self-conscious and slightly embarrassed. This awkward appendage, with its avocado stains and ragged edges, told the world, *I'm not okay.* But towards the end, much as I looked forward to its removal, I could see how--if I had to--I could get along. I became a little less clumsy. My dog licked it from time to time, signaling to me that my cast had become part of myself. *So maybe I'm not okay,* I began to think. And that's all right. Frustration behind me, hope ahead, life, once again, is good.

Resources used to prepare this sermon include Michael J. Fox, *Lucky Man* (New York: Hyperion, 2002); Copyright © 2002 Michael J. Fox. Reprinted by permission of Hyperion. The reading from Pema Chödron is in an anthology titled *Prayers for a Thousand Years*, ed. Elizabeth Roberts and Elias Amidon (Harper: SanFrancisco, 1999). Thank you to Joyce Holmen for the words to Fred Small's song "Talking Wheelchair Blues." Fred's website is <http://jg.org/folk/artists/fredsmall/fred_small.html>.

FINDING HOME

THE ART OF BELONGING

January 8, 1995

It may seem presumptuous, but I think I know how many of you are feeling about being here today. Especially if you are a newcomer--just to be here, in the sanctuary, taking part in a Sunday morning service, comes as a shock. You swore off religion a long time ago. You could not reconcile your personal feelings with the faith of your childhood. Or you had no faith in your childhood and never went to services of any kind, so even in a simple service like this one, you spend most of your time anxiously preparing for what comes next: is it sitting down, or standing up? Singing or silence? Just coming here for the first or second time requires all your energy and courage. There's a dialogue going on in your head. Even as you listen to the words and the music, other voices noisily debate whether this is the place for you--or not.

When we come to a religious community as adults, we come with our doubts, our wounds, our defenses, and our ambivalence. There is no other way to get here. The path is full of obstacles. For many--perhaps most--of us, our ambivalence never entirely goes away. Even committed members of this community, who have given generously of themselves for many years, still attest to their doubts and their conflicts over keeping the faith.

I might even go so far as to say that we Unitarian Universalists maintain, perhaps with some outlaw pride, our ambivalence, our skepticism, and our sense of alienation, the way other religious folks maintain a regular reading of scripture, a disciplined acceptance of belief, and traditional liturgies in ancient languages. We seek out the margins of the religious landscape. We fill in the pews on Sunday morning, from the back to the front, and stay on the edge for a good long time.

In typical off-beat Unitarian Universalist fashion, I approached my ministry training the same way. I arrived at Divinity School in the middle of the year, commuted to Cambridge from my post-Woodstock nation homestead in Central Massachusetts for the first six months, took the introductory Bible courses during my last year, not my first, and when commencement day arrived, I was long gone, already at work at my first church in New Jersey. The Dean of Students once commented to me after I'd been there for a while, that I could stop camping out, as it looked like I was going to stay. So I moved to a town that was only twenty minutes away from school instead of an hour and a half, and started playing the piano for the chapel services. A big commitment.

As a minister, I've since had to make deeper and deeper commitments to my life in the Unitarian Universalist community. Those commitments have been good for me. But I always notice how quickly I lapse into that characteristically tentative posture: just last week at our Sunday service, I sat in the next to last pew as always. I want to be there, but I need to know I'm not trapped.

Back in the 60's the Unitarian Universalists ran a very successful print ad campaign. The following words appeared in a small box in newspapers, anywhere but on the religion page: "You may be a Unitarian without knowing it," they declared. I was brought up in a Unitarian Universalist household, so I would recognize the ads with familiarity, and a combination of pride and embarrassment: pride because the fringe sect to which I feared we belonged actually made it into the newspaper from time to time, making it slightly more legitimate; embarrassment because our faith was apparently so weak that people could practice it without even knowing they were doing so. My brothers and I used to laugh at this modest attempt to evangelize just a little, to draw people to our church by appealing to their absence of intentionality instead of trying to induce it. Interestingly enough, this has been the most successful advertising campaign we have ever run.

It is part of who we are as a religious community to be searching for our own unique ways of affiliating, even if that doesn't look like what we are doing. There is always a tension and an ambivalence for us when we enter into the realm of religion, for we believe, quite correctly, that religious authenticity is something to be guarded with vigilance and to be tested always. Even once we discover that there is a place where we might belong, there are layers of resistance and doubt, and patterns of self-styled individualism to accommodate on the way to making a commitment to something as official as membership.

Becoming a member of any group naturally compromises our individually self-defined norms. When we are only concerned with ourselves, we don't need to negotiate or to accept the disappointing along with the good. When we commit ourselves to any relationship, intimate, familial, or spiritual, the tensions increase, but so do the rewards. Spiritual commitments raise higher tensions for us Unitarian Universalists. They also deliver greater rewards, because we are more honest with ourselves and with each other about our *religious* doubts, wounds, and fears than we are about almost any other aspect of our lives. Authenticity arises out of this ambivalence, revealing our own true selves, struggling, like refugees, for freedom.

We *are* refugees, most of us, coming into this faith late and wary. I've never had a reason to think about our chalice this way before, but I would guess that the reason why we accepted it as the symbol of our community has nothing to do with the chalice or the flame--indeed, some of you have accepted it *despite* the fact that it is a chalice, with associations to the Last Supper, the Holy Grail, and other artifacts of Christianity. The reason why we accepted it is because it was a means by which our community was able to help people fleeing persecution. We identify with that part of our tradition which helps refugees, which acts for no reason other than that it was the right thing to do, which is all our faith ultimately requires of each of us. Refugees helping refugees: it sounds like home to me.

In contrast to that bit of *our* history, the story of Noah and the Ark, which explores new territory in the relationship between the Hebrew people and their God, may be required reading for those of us who believe that it is good to know something about the Hebrew and Christian scripture, but it is not *our* story at all. I cannot imagine Unitarian Universalists pairing off obediently, leaving others to contend with a tragic fate. I cannot imagine Unitarian Universalists believing in a God who would let such a catastrophe befall all but a few chosen ones. I cannot imagine Unitarian Universalists sitting it out, away from the action, until God sends us a rainbow.

I do not see us in that story, but that story can help us see ourselves. For we are clearly on the side of those who do *not* feel chosen, whose fates are determined by human morality, who struggle to survive, and are ultimately transformed by their own history. That is the story of refugees who make it to safety. It is also the story for so many of us who find sanctuary here in this room with each other.

Belonging to a religious community is not a simple straightforward matter for us. Belonging is an art: the art of transforming the past into something true, something real, something to make us whole. Given our naturally alienated stance and our tentative approach to faith, the tensions that arise in us simply walking through the doors of this meeting room, or trying on this new religious identity--Unitarian Universalist--which seems to take so much explaining, we approach membership cautiously, looking for ways to be part of things without having to make a decision about commitment.

Some people choose to remain perpetual visitors. We can understand why: given who we are, most of us feel like visitors ourselves. But for those who make the commitment to joining a congregation, to claiming their Unitarian Universalist identity, to deepening their ties to others, the hope of transformation assumes reality, and what we call faith begins to work.

Whatever our life story, whatever our origins, one of the great achievements of being alive is the possibility of integrating everything about ourselves, good or bad, into who we can become. We take the early childhood hurts, the gigantic embarrassing mistakes and the notable failures, and instead of pushing them away, we let them teach us and tell us what we need to learn. Fulfillment in life does not come simply from accruing one success after another; fulfillment comes from letting no experience be wasted, not even the ones which threaten our very being. For in using everything we are given, and in using it with honesty and compassion for our human condition, we come into our own true selves.

Transformation comes from making and keeping good commitments. Through our loyalty, our continuity, and our love, we slowly shape ourselves according to the promises we keep. When it comes to a religious community, making good commitments is our *reason* for being together. We cannot experience the fulfillment of this faith if we make no commitment to it, for our faith is in the depth of our belonging.

To join this congregation is to accept the invitation to be transformed according to the vision which has inspired generations of seekers, a safe place to call our religious home. It is a serious step, especially for us, because commitments like these are not ones we take lightly, but it is also a tender gesture of hope, for the life which so many of us thought we could never have--a life of faith as we choose to define it--unflinchingly, with all our faculties, the intuitive as well as the rational, teaching us the truth about who we are and what life can ultimately mean. Refugees from the varied confines of religious orthodoxy, we know what we need when we want to be safe and free. It's what we can have here, if each of us offers ourselves to the vision that is ready to emerge.

And that vision delivers safety not because it is cut off from the world or from our doubts about what it is possible to believe. It delivers because of all that is welcome: our need to be in the world, side by side with all the other refugees and seekers; our doubts and our ambivalence, which are our test of truth; our own true selves, whoever we are, growing stronger as we learn from life together; and our tender hope, that such commitments as the one we make to this community can make real the future we desire and the people we want to become. For the vision, and for the hope, we belong to one another. May we be transformed in the image of that vision. May we be whole and free, safe in the knowledge that where we are going is exactly where we need to be.

THE TRANSFORMING SPIRIT

May 21, 2000

A recent, rare visit to the hardware store--a place about as mysterious to me as the catacombs--led me to question what spirituality means to us, and why so many people seem to be seeking it these days. I was searching for non-toxic drain cleaner, when the owner of the store approached me to offer help. After a brief discussion of the comparative merits of drain cleaners, he came out with a startling comment. "I can see you are a very spiritual person," he said, "I can see it in your eyes."

I flushed with the uneasy self-conscious feeling I always have whenever anyone talks to me about the way I look. And it struck me how odd it was for one stranger to say something like that to another. I admit I was flattered. Warming up, I introduced myself, not wanting to miss an opportunity to tell someone about the church, offering it as validation of his uncanny ability to spot a minister.

Driving home, I thought about how loosely people talk about spirituality these days. Spirituality is everywhere. The diversity alone is a positive feature--popular books abound on every religious tradition, mainstream and esoteric, there seems to be something for everyone. It wouldn't be there if we did not need it. And yet, it always makes me wonder why the pervasiveness of spirituality has not made the world a more humane place.

Nicolaus Mills, American Studies scholar and author of a recent book, *The Triumph of Meanness,* observes that the world is becoming crueler. Self-interest has become an acceptable social value. We share the impression that we live in a hostile environment, and our response is to look after ourselves and our families, forming armor against what threatens us. Overwhelmed, perhaps, by the enormity of the world's social problems, and frightened by the risks of involvement, many people have shut down the part of themselves that tries to comprehend what we are up against.

Our spiritual yearnings often appear to be a response to the pain of being alive in a world that does not make us feel better. Spiritual seeking is a consolation, a shot at a better, alternative reality in which to live and grow and learn. We gently encourage each other to follow whatever path leads us to inner peace, and who can blame us, when all around us there is unrest. If we can gain from our effort even a small measure of healing and insight, then life becomes that much easier to bear.

Meanwhile, though, the world continues its grim downward spin into selfishness, greed, and fragmentation. Nicolaus Mills writes that our pessimism and our reluctance to envision a better world virtually guarantee that we will never have one. The "real and symbolic fortress" in which we live today, with its message, "I'll take care of me and mine," is a terminally self-defeating stance against what we have given up trying to change.

Though our spiritual practices may offer us an image of reality we like better than the one in which we must commute to work, we cannot afford to abandon the real world if we have any hope left that it will ever improve. According to Mills, the only hope we have is the one we can build in our voluntary associations--from bowling clubs to religious institutions, only the power of community can coax us out of our cocoons and back into action where we are needed. Chipping away at the "I'll take care of me and mine" mentality by encountering other people in places without security fences, or psychic armor, community is the path we walk towards a better world.

Individual experiences of affiliating with a community, such as our church, vary widely in some respects and yet are strikingly similar in others. Some people, who want to break down the barriers they see between themselves and others, carefully and intentionally research the place they eventually choose. Others have an intuitive feeling that they need to belong somewhere, not unlike the butterflies that emerge from their cocoons saying "gotta go, gotta go," not really knowing why, just knowing it's right. Still others find that self-sufficiency cannot sustain them through grief or loneliness, or through the rigors of raising a family, without companionship and empathy.

Whatever the initial impulse, people move towards community because there is engagement with life and people, and it gives them a vision of hope. Hope to make friends, hope to survive a rough patch of time, hope to find a way to make the world a better place: without it, there is no future. Communities engender hope, a powerful transforming human impulse to envision that what may come next, the next day or the next decade, is worth our work and our struggle.

This hope is more than an individual feeling. It is a shared vision of a better world. It is what draws us out of ourselves and calls us to act on the transcendent values that give our lives meaning: justice, equality, dignity, respect.

As I think back to the hardware store, I get the uneasy feeling that all our glib talk about spirituality, and our restless flitting from one spiritual trend to another, are signs of what is both good and bad about the times in which we live. It's good because spirituality runs through daily life; it's accessible, diverse, and democratic in essence. Why shouldn't people talk about their spiritual lives on television talk shows, or in hardware stores, for that matter? It's bad, however, because we run the risk of believing that spirituality is a safe haven from the rest of life, a way to avoid living up to our human calling to make the world a better place. It's good if it brings people together to talk about their true selves. It's bad if it is just another opportunity for people to posture and compete with each other.

Spirituality is simply a name for all the ways in which we respond to the mystery of life, the various images we make, by training and temperament, of meaning and value, the truths that we sense but cannot grasp as a whole. Like the butterflies that emerge out of their cocoons, not knowing why but only that they "gotta go," we live and die within a cycle that is larger than we are, and which we experience in our own instinctive and human manner. Some of us will try to contain the mystery, or to explain it, or to organize it; others will leave it alone, but these are choices that reveal more about who we are than about what it is.

Our spirituality is our human version of "gotta go," the way we speak of things we know in ways we cannot fully articulate. And that is why much of today's spirituality falls short of its potential. In the mad dash to grasp what is essentially mysterious and unknowable, we accept partial answers that claim to be whole, leaving us partial and falling short too.

It doesn't have to be that way. The full potential of spirituality is to *make* us whole, to integrate who we are with our intuitive understanding of life and our desire to contribute meaningfully to it. It calls forth the transcendent values and vision of a better world that it is our human nature to construct. It gives us hope and energy to offset hostile and destructive forces in modern society. It causes us to value our relationships to one another, not to undermine them. It makes us better people.

That is why belonging to a community is a spiritual path. Our comings and goings, rites of passage and annual meetings, are the spiritual practice of community. Community thrives on vision, and nurtures our values. It offers us hope. It remembers us when we are gone.

Those who take community as their spiritual path walk through life with others, as loosely or tightly connected as they need to be. They find themselves doing things that surprise them--working with children, speaking in public, meditating in silence, and they grow from the experience. The daily life of community is complex and often messy, requiring humor, forgiveness and patience. But these things make us better people. So we don't let go of the vision of a place where the dignity, worth, and potential of all people are given and grow. Banding together, we see how much we can do, and the injustices of the world cannot stop us from making a difference. Then we are whole, and living up to the full potential our spiritual practice teaches us to seek.

The next time I need to go to the hardware store--not too soon, I hope--I will remember to tell the man there what I think it means to be spiritual. I'll tell him I am a minister because this community is my spiritual path. I'll tell him I have no more understanding of the mystery of life than anyone else I know. And I'll invite him to come to our church, where spiritual longings become human bonds, and no one is really a stranger.

Resources used to prepare this sermon include Nicolaus Mills, *The Triumph of Meanness* (Boston: Houghton Mifflin, 1997); and Sam Swope, *Gotta Go! Gotta Go!* (New York: Farrar, Straus and Giroux, 2000).

THE LONELINESS THAT IS LOS ANGELES

February 21, 1999

You never know what will happen to a sermon on the way to Sunday morning. This one I intended to be a meditation on the character of Los Angeles, and how we are shaped by it. I had in mind the image of a vast urban desert, where forces of nature converge with forces of human nature, all slightly out of control, yielding a distinctive, individualistic spirit and strength. What is in one sense loneliness is in another sense freedom, the room to run wild in a place where nobody knows you anyway.

What I did not expect, however, was that while you were waiting for me to get this sermon together--this is the one that had to be postponed from January--many of you would tell me how much you wanted to hear about loneliness. You were not hoping to hear about freedom or the advantages of urban anonymity, but rather about the sense of dislocation so many of you feel, and how to remedy it. Your poignant comments corrected my approach to the topic of the day.

What we have here is not some bracing brave new world but a place where too many people simply do not feel at home. The description I read earlier in the service from James Howard Kuntsler's *The Geography of Nowhere* all too accurately describes an environment that is full of jarring contrasts and disconnects. They jangle our nerves. We race from place to place, madly trying to connect the dots, but they don't connect; we live amid contradictions that we prefer not to see; we try to tie it all together inside, but nothing happens.

This is the familiar pessimistic view about life here that we have learned to love. It has a perverse appeal, especially for anxious people like me. Finally I get to live somewhere that engages my catastrophic imagination to the limit, so that instead of simply being anxious that something might happen, here, it actually does happen. Mike Davis ups the ante even more in his recent work *The Ecology of*

Fear. He writes, "Recent research ... has transformed the question 'Why so many recent disasters?' into the truly unnerving question 'Why so few?'" That's what I want to know, too.

I am continually jolted by what I see all around me here; so I remain vigilant and alert; I feel strangely alive. This is the mystique of Los Angeles: it's not for sissies, as we declared after the Northridge earthquake. It's a visually and psychologically arduous state of mind that produces plenty of adrenaline and masks a lot of the pain.

All the hyperactivity of our lives and the constant depiction of our city in movies and TV have only added to the mystique. Everyone can recognize Los Angeles, even those who have never been here. When you actually drive down San Vicente Boulevard or walk on the Santa Monica Pier, you have the funny feeling you were here in another life.

A pervasive sense of unreality arises not only because this place is visually familiar. It is also visually shocking. Here you can live in a condominium building adorned with the sculpture of a giant transvestite clown. Evocative fantasy facades are slapped on the fronts of apartment houses that are actually just stucco boxes. The first year I lived here I rented an apartment in a nondescript building off Wilshire Boulevard; you couldn't tell that on the inside was a magnificent green courtyard, a hidden oasis that I now realize is so typical of the private beauty many here possess.

Amid the ugliness, humor, and beauty jammed together in uncoordinated and chaotic groupings that are barely neighborhoods, we contemplate our condition and see how alone we are. Our city evolved according to patterns dictated by the need to move water, railroads, and eventually cars, and not by the human need to be connected. With everyone moving about so much, few hours are actually spent at home anyway. The usual patterns of connecting to others, through children, schools, neighbors, shopping, do not occur naturally for many of us. Rather everything we do is intentional-- thought out, scheduled, self-selected--and often, alone. The kind of contact we would take for granted in some other places simply never happens here unless we will it. That seems like a lonely way to live.

And yet, ask anyone who is living in a comfortable, settled enclave offering all the expected relationships and patterns of community and you are just as likely to hear about loneliness there as you are here. Other people in other places don't associate their loneliness with where they live in quite the same way we do, however. They feel lonely if they lack meaningful, intimate connections to other people. That can happen to anyone anywhere. That is also what happens to us here, but somehow, it just feels different because we are here. What enthralls us about Los Angeles is the belief that it is different somehow, that it is a place with unique side effects, special effects, even. H.L. Mencken named it "Los Angeles the Damned," which is one way of being special. Even earlier, at the turn of the century, out-of-town visitors would fall under the spell of the "climate, the fruits and the flowers," as Henry James said he did, and pronounce that Los Angeles stood apart from all other places by "a delicious difference."

How well I remember, my last icy winter back in Boston, the fantasies I stoked about being warm, about being outside, about being somewhere totally different from where I was. That "delicious difference" still draws us, whether we move here from New England or El Salvador.

Much of the heightened awareness we acquire when we move here--and most of us did move here from somewhere else--comes from our sense that something will be different now. That is the image Los Angeles cultivates about itself; it is what most of us embrace when we arrive; it drives up our expectations, and it sets up our disappointments. Perhaps it's time to stop believing the hype about LA, and take charge of making it into a place where we all can feel more at home. You do need some special skills to survive. You don't need to know how to scrape the ice off your windshield, at least not at the lower elevations, but you do need to know how to motivate yourself to join a community. You don't need to take on this entire vast city as a whole in order to feel at home here, but you do need to make a few close friends if you plan to stay. This is a city that will present you with a dazzling array of options--too many options--unless you make choices that reflect your principles and your values. You do need to know what your principles and values are.

This vast and diverse landscape offers such a rich experience, though, that the work it takes to be at home here is worth it. James Howard Kuntsler's description of the contrasts between the vaulting mountain and ocean vistas and the "bleak, monotonous, decaying" streetscape of the flatlands is daunting, but it provokes us into learning what we need by looking around where we are. The lesson is two-fold. There is inspiration and uplift in nature here, and if we ever forget that, we really are doomed. We inhabit an environment of unparalleled beauty and accessibility that we enjoy regularly, despite the occasional reminder that Mother Earth has a mind of her own. Don't lose sight of the beauty that surrounds us. Go outside and be in it. We also need to go *inside*. I remember how struck I was by the fact that my modest, bland apartment building contained within it a lush green garden that kept the air moist and the inner courtyard serene. It's a good image to remind us all how much of the beauty here is hidden away in the interiors; you need to make a little effort to find it. The short view of blighted neighborhoods, distressed communities and depressed people that James Howard Kuntsler described in his essay on LA is what you get when you don't look inside. To appreciate the beauty that lasts as long as you need it, you have to look inside.

And *when* you look inside yourself and find a lonely person, you don't have to accept that this is all you can be. Inside each of you is a beautiful garden, waiting to be discovered and enjoyed by others. Cultivate yourself within and venture out.

Los Angeles is a fast-moving and far-flung human community that presents special challenges and rewards to those who choose to live here. The distances may be great but where else can you live among so many cultures, hear their languages, eat their food, learn their customs, and see your children make friends with each other? The mix we have here simply doesn't happen in settled, conventional places. Yes, we must reach out to each other. Yes, we must look past the facades and into the gardens within. That is what it takes to be at home.

Our yearning for home has expressed itself in every imaginable way, especially in the diversity of spiritual communities we find here. Though the religion of the indigenous people and the missions that came much later were all that was here for a long time, once the area became populated with newcomers, all manner of faiths sprang up. The 1940 *WPA Guide to Los Angeles* claimed, "The multiplicity and diversity of faiths that flourish in the aptly named City of Angels probably cannot be duplicated in any other city on earth." That is more true today than ever.

What accounts for this enormous appetite for religion I cannot say for certain. Perhaps it has to do with the loneliness we associate with being here, a desire to be at home in ourselves and in our world that cannot be met except in community with others. The desire to connect with other people at a deep level is a religious impulse. It is an affirmation of the garden within, the beauty all around us, and the need to venture out into the world to become part of something that is larger than ourselves. Religious communities invite us to reach out *and* look inside; as diverse as they may be, they all serve the same ultimate purpose: to remind us that we are not alone.

For many of us in Los Angeles, our religious community is our primary affiliation--the one place where we are known and accepted as we are, where connections can be made and we can pull ourselves together. If you have chosen the Unitarian Universalist community, then you know how good it is to find this beautiful green garden thriving on the care of thoughtful people whose principles and values you share. Come inside, and let it nurture you. There is no reason, any more, to feel alone. The city is large, anyone can get lost; but here, among strangers and friends, you can let yourself be found and be at home with one another.

Resources used to prepare this sermon include James Howard Kuntsler, *The Geography of Nowhere* (New York: Touchstone, 1993); Mike Davis, *Ecology of Fear: Los Angeles and the Imagination of Disaster* (New York: Henry Holt, 1998); and the 1940 *WPA Guide to Los Angeles.*

THE GROUND OF OUR BEING

October 5, 1997

When I moved to Southern California just over four years ago, I was seeking, as so many others have too, a new landscape to explore and a new frame of reference to use in understanding my life. It's an adjustment I've made in stages, not all at once, but gradually, images and viewpoints do shift. One shift I've pursued consciously is to read and learn about Western writers and thinkers who evoke and express the experience of living here, and who have helped shaped the culture because they did. It is a varied, idiosyncratic group that has taken up residence in my imagination. Some of them have made an appearance in sermons: Swami Yogananda, John Muir, Jacob Needleman, and, most recently, Christopher Isherwood. Others have been less public, occupying space once taken up by various New England eccentrics and divines such as Alice and William James, Ralph Waldo Emerson, Bronson Alcott, and their like, who dominated my imagination in the past. Now I have so much more in common with my new imaginary friends, the old ones have been displaced. But that's what I wanted: a big shift.

One shift I could never have predicted was the shifting and heaving we experienced in the Northridge earthquake of January, 1994. It left a lasting impact on us all in one way or another.

Many of you faced major home repairs. Here at the church, our bungalow on 17th Street was damaged *beyond* repair. The bungalow became a neighborhood eyesore, and painful reminder of our various displacements, until it was finally demolished this summer. Here in the sanctuary the walls cracked, the fireplace buckled, and what had been a newly refurbished worship space needed refurbishing all over again. Just thinking about the mess makes me anxious.

John Muir happened to be camping in Yosemite when he felt an earthquake's "strange thrilling motion" roll across the forest floor. As Muir wrote in his journal, it provided the "sublime spectacle of an avalanche of boulders pouring ... in an arc of glowing, passionate fire, perfumed the air with crushed spruce, and blanketed the valley with a luminous, moonlit dust cloud." This proof of the "orderly beauty-making love-beats of Nature's heart" left him "both glad and frightened." Such an idealized view of a natural, but terrifying event may be difficult for us to sustain for very long, especially once we know the damage and human suffering it can cause.

But Muir's response seems spontaneous and innocent, and his idealizing seems preferable to the indifference, or perhaps denial, of Alice B. Toklas's father, "who, when told San Francisco had been rocked by an earthquake and was on fire, replied, 'That will give us a black eye in the east,' and went back to sleep."

These two responses neatly summarize the dominant attitudes that have shaped California's relationship to nature. We are torn between a fanatic reverence for everything natural, wild and free, and a callous compartmentalization of reality to suit our own purposes. Every now and then the two converge, as in the case of the jogger who said that she accelerated as she ran through the freeway underpass, thinking, "Not now, please." I do that every time I head up the ramp to the 405 North, or drive over those ominous bumps on the 10 East near La Cienega. We all have our bargaining moments with earthquake probability.

"Not now, please." The rest of the time, we vacillate among the varied attitudes of bravado, denial, fear, awe, and acceptance. But unlike the patients Kübler-Ross studied as they underwent their final illness, there is no one to reassure us that what we are feeling is appropriate and normal. In California, who can tell?

I visited a special exhibit at the Huntington recently, depicting the history of delivering water to our semi-arid desert of Los Angeles. With the cavalier but seductive advertising slogan, "We need it ... let's go get it!" the Metropolitan Water District secured the funding for the Colorado River aqueduct. "We need it ... let's go get it!" summarizes the craven opportunism that has exploited and imperiled our environment, but it also voices the unabashed spirit of pioneers and immigrants who were spunky enough to get here and enterprising enough to "get it," that is to say, whatever piece of the California Dream they dreamed to claim for themselves. It's not all bad.

And yet, underneath this energy and hope lies a much more powerful and unpredictable force, the force of nature. An earthquake here, an El Niño there, and all we have left is rubble and broken dreams.

Is this something to take seriously, or simply to catalog along with everything else, the absurd, the tragic, and the new, that happens here? "I am sure that sooner or later everything conceivable happens once or twice in California," writes communitarian visionary Amitai Etzioni.

So am I. I think that's why we're all still here. The possibilities just seem endless. And yet, like Daniel doomed to perish in the lion's den, our susceptibility to catastrophe seems inevitable. Earthquakes will happen here, on faults we know and, as in the case of the Northridge quake, faults we don't know. We can blithely assume, as Thurston Clarke says most Californians do, that whatever happens, we will be among the lucky survivors, or we can come to grips with what the future is really asking of us.

Although most of us would not want to admit it now, the Northridge earthquake was terrifying, especially if you lived in an area that really rocked and swayed when it hit. For months after, we all experienced the jumpiness caused by unpredictable aftershocks, and the memory of having been awakened in the night. Depression ensued, especially for those who had to move out of their homes or manage expensive and disruptive repairs.

You may not appreciate this reminder--like most Californians, we want to forget the terror as quickly as possible--but there are lessons we can learn from that experience now that we are well beyond it. And we *are* rugged survivors. I remember how delighted I was to see the first post-earthquake T-shirt, proclaiming "LA is not for sissies" in bold letters across the front. Nature may be harsh here, but we are strong.

Another lesson has to do with fear and our need for others. One response to the earthquake here was that people joined the church. The vulnerability we all felt made us more aware of how much we needed each other. When the Great Earthquake hit San Francisco in 1906, Stanford professor William Jarvis "popularized the concept of 'earthquake love,' defining it as a 'tenderness' toward others who shared the experience, and an 'uplift from the common lot that briefly banished loneliness.'" We had our own version of that experience here. Some neighborhoods and housing complexes transformed themselves into communities after the Northridge quake; but it did not happen everywhere. What was universal was the need we all felt to reach out to each other.

Thurston Clarke traveled the San Andreas Fault from Eureka to the Salton Sea. Along the way, he encountered many examples of the California Dream now corrupted and bankrupt of possibilities. "We need it--let's go and get it" has left its mark on people's souls as well as on the landscape.

But that was not all he encountered. He found people like us, "eccentric community builders simply thick on the ground in California, as hard to miss as the scars left by the San Andreas." Well, they weren't all like us, but you'd recognize them: people who nurture a Dream that "incorporated California's tolerance, love of nature, and optimism;" a Dream to replace "an antiquated Dream based on unlimited resources and material rewards that is becoming increasingly difficult to deliver as California sprawls and grows."

The Dream is one of deep-rooted community, one that can "withstand the destruction of material possessions," which is likely to happen when the Big One finally happens. We can build a firm foundation of human community that will hold us even when the ground lets loose underneath. We can, if our being is grounded in something deeper. While William James, the psychologist from Boston, was lecturing at Stanford in 1906, the Great San Francisco earthquake hit. It woke him up in his shaking bed. "He hurried to the station and caught the only train making a run into San Francisco that day," Thurston Clarke reports. "For hours he wandered through the rubble, impressed by the 'universal equanimity' of the survivors, and reporting that 'the terms *awful* and *dreadful* fell often enough from people's lips, but always with a sort of abstract meaning, and with a face that seemed to admire the vastness of the catastrophe.'"

In 1994 we all found different ways to make friends with the earthquake (at least that was how it felt for me). What helped me was to remember that this was not some alien force, maliciously robbing us of sleep and security. Rather it was a great and powerful force of creation as well as destruction, and I needed to make peace with it, ride the wave, adapt. Gentle Daniel made friends with the lion as well as the lamb. So must we find a way to live with nature. We may not ever be on terms as intimate as John Muir, who spoke affectionately of the "orderly beauty-making love-beats of Nature's heart" when he first felt them. But we may open *our* hearts to a way of life that teaches us our place in creation.

"We need it--let's go get it" won't work for us any longer. Unless we're talking about the need for community, for values grounded in an ethic of care and love of neighbor, and the need for a gentle faith that allows us to sleep, at night, at peace with the natural forces of creation.

Some of my old heroes from the past, like Alice James or Ralph Waldo Emerson, were people whose self-knowledge was staggering and whose imaginations were relentless in their originality. But they, like their friend Bronson Alcott, never made their peace with nature.

Alice James became a reclusive invalid; Emerson, although he wrote eloquently about nature, refused to go camping with John Muir when he made his trip out west; and Bronson Alcott, who could have made the California varsity squad of eccentrics, found the New England winters too harsh to support his vegetarian commune. Sadly, he simply moved back to the suburbs of Boston when it failed. Perhaps he should have come out here. As people I'm sure I have short-shrifted their memory, but as role models in my mind they needed to be replaced with hardy, adventurous Western types with new ideas and a dream to pursue. Those new people, as compelling as the swamis and John Muir and Christopher Isherwood all were, are also the people I see here every day.

Every one of us living here in this semi-arid desert shot through with faults, grounds our being in a reality that has never lost its beauty, its hope, or its potential to fulfill us. So long as we remember that what we need most in life is that which withstands every quake and storm: each other's care, and a reverence for all of creation.

The following resource was used to prepare this sermon: Amitai Etzioni, *The Spirit of Community: The Reinvention of American Society* (New York: Simon & Schuster, 1993). John Muir, Alice B. Toklas's father, and William Jarvis are quoted in Thurston Clarke, *California Fault: Searching for the Spirit of a State Along the San Andreas* (New York: Ballantine Books, 1996).

THE SPIRIT MOVES WEST

The Unitarian Fellowship of the Desert

April 17, 1994

While Ralph Waldo Emerson was writing his first set of essays, trouble was heating up on the Texas-Mexico border, and the larger question of annexation, the appropriation of Mexican land by the United States, had yet to be settled in a bloody war. Emerson himself speculated that legislating the vast expanse of the west would be difficult, given the variety and harshness of the terrain. His more politically minded friends at Brook Farm opposed our "plundering aggression" on Mexico, and all agreed with Emerson that the Puritan conscience would judge such an invasion as immoral.

Some thirty years later, Emerson made a trip to the West. While in California, Emerson wrote to his friend Thomas Carlyle that he was amazed by the weather--"day after day for six weeks of uninterrupted sunshine"--the trip appears to have been a success. Interestingly enough, besides the usual calls on transplanted Unitarians from the east, Emerson also sought brief encounters with icons of the western spirit: Brigham Young and John Muir. John Muir invited him to go camping with him, but Emerson declined, preferring to spend the night indoors at an inn. Not many of Emerson's words survive this trip--only a letter to Thomas Carlyle and a few journal notes he jotted down after he returned home to Concord. So we cannot speculate much about the meaning of this pilgrimage. But Emerson's moves suggest that he was at least as interested in Brigham Young and John Muir as he was in the transplanted culture of the east. His instincts were good. I think he saw what I would have wanted him to see.

I've only been a resident of California for nine months. Any pronouncements I can make about the west are certain only to haunt and embarrass me in years to come, so I have chosen to speak about Emerson instead. But I have to say a few words about my own first impressions. A year ago, while I was visiting Santa Monica and wondering how I would fit in there, two apparently unchanging realities kept me company, the sunshine and the New York accents on the local public radio station. Now, having lived through nine months and an earthquake, rain, floods, and fires, I consider myself no longer an outsider, but there is still a lot to learn. Some of what I have learned is about myself: how I am more conventional than I thought, and am sometimes startled--even aghast--at the free-wheeling, individualistic, and traditionless culture I have encountered here; and at the same time, how quickly and positively I have embraced that same freedom, knowing, instinctively, like others have known, that it helps me to be more myself.

Jacob Needleman, professor of philosophy at San Francisco State, has written insightfully about the spiritual condition of the west. He writes "as a Californian, a man without tradition who hears all around him claims of a spiritual revolution being made not only by the representatives of alien traditions but by countless people like himself who have hardly ever felt the breath of traditional spirituality in their lives." He goes on, "Without much real concern for the historical background, many of these thousands see the present moment as the beginning of a new age: they are confident the future will be different from the past."

Freedom from the past has nurtured a spiritual diversity in the west, along with some very strange gods. In Los Angeles, ethnic diversity accounts for the proliferation of various faiths, established by missionaries from their countries of origin. But there is so much more: from the Crystal Cathedral of Orange County to the Pentecostal store fronts to the clandestine experiments with LSD in the home of Aldous Huxley, the search for enlightenment has taken all shapes and forms here, leading one writer, David Reid, to ask, "What is it about [California] that inflames so many prophetic souls?" I don't know.

I do know that Emerson and his Transcendentalist friends caught a glimmering of that spirit. There is an affinity between Emerson's strident affirmations of the self, of freedom from tradition, and of the human ability to see and to know God; an affinity between that distinctively New England creation and what has become the spiritual culture of California. And what is interesting about that is that Emerson, of course, was a *Unitarian* minister; most of his Transcendentalist friends were Unitarians too, and we modern day Unitarian Universalists living in California, trying to make sense of who we are and where we are, may find something to guide us here that comes from our own tradition.

Not that Emerson would have cared, I suppose. He made a career for himself out of leaving the church, defining himself and his thought against the prevailing attitudes of Unitarianism, and once having left the ministry, never fully identifying himself with us again. He found Unitarian preaching lifeless, lacking evidence of personal experience, betraying "diffidence, fear of innovation, too much respect for authority, custom, and inherited opinion." Of course, Emerson found his audience largely among these same people, all seeking their safe rebellions from tradition, while never moving many miles from each other.

Emerson did not choose to join Brook Farm or other experiments in living advocated by some of his friends. But he was patient and supportive of those whose enthusiasm led them to communal living. And the Emerson household was rarely without long-term visitors--Margaret Fuller, Henry Thoreau, and the Bronson Alcott family. Bronson Alcott was the father of Louisa May Alcott, whose idyllic depiction of family life in *Little Women* bore no resemblance to the perennially doomed pursuits of her real family. Bronson Alcott was a dreamer and an idealist, whose experimental vegetarian homestead, "Fruitlands," barely made it six months, until they abandoned it, hungry, during a harsh New England winter.

Of such adventures Emerson seems to have been tolerant, only occasionally complaining about his friends: "Their whole doctrine is spiritual, but they always end with saying, 'Give us much land & money.' If I should give them anything it should be facility & not beneficence." Interesting to note that Bronson Alcott deplored the west, and declared, after a visit to St. Louis, how little he had in common with "the wild life of the west." These were complicated people.

I have never been very interested in Emerson and the Transcendentalists before now. At their worst, they seemed to me to be opportunists, working over their religion and their neighborhood with their rebellious posturing. Some--Margaret Fuller and Theodore Parker, for example--took real risks with their lives and broke away from their cultured confines. Others, like Emerson and Thoreau, conducted lives that seemed to me safe and derivative, despite their bold pronouncements. But now, re-reading Emerson's work in California, I discover in myself an appreciation for his originality and a compassion for his life.

His contribution to Unitarianism is undeniable. It was Emerson who led us to affirm that inside each of us was the source of religious experience and spiritual authority: no one can tell us what to believe. And it was Emerson who encouraged us to seek God not in tradition, not in church, not in books, but in ourselves and in the experiences of our own lives. If these are the two things every Unitarian Universalist understands about our common faith, they both come straight from Emerson.

Perhaps it is closer to the truth for me to say that my scorn of Emerson came not from a judgment that his life might be safe and derivative, but rather from a fear that without some changes, it was *my* life that was not really my own. For what else is it, than the desire to start over, to be released from the past, to be authentic and free, that brings so many of us here to the west anyway?

Looking back at my life in Boston from my new perspective in Santa Monica, I see someone whose entire adult aspirations were defined on one side of the river, by Harvard, and fulfilled on the other side, by Beacon Hill. My favorite restaurant was in the building where Margaret Fuller and her friends edited and published the Transcendentalist journal, *The Dial*. It was as if I was unconsciously retracing the steps of my religious, though not genetic, forebears, while not really wanting to be on their path--while wanting, instead, to be on my *own* path. And now, I find myself in the land of strange gods, making hospital calls across the street from the big blue Scientology headquarters, visiting hot springs with my colleagues down the road from Krishnamurti's home, learning meditation from a Catholic spiritual director, and finding my own way. I had already been living here for several months when I remembered that Aldous Huxley was an idol from my childhood; I have read every one of his books--how could I have forgotten that? But I remembered it here.

Whatever it is that living in the west will come to mean for me, it seems that I have begun with what Emerson has had to teach me. There is something unique and inviolate about the integrity within each of us; if we can remember that, and act on it, and call it holy--we have discovered something more precious than can be found anywhere else. And it is freedom.

It's the freedom that comes from who we are right now, not what our history has been. Not the history of the west, either--after understanding how so much of this land was taken away from other people, whose oppression served others' need for a frontier. But rather, what we have become: it is the richness of the surviving cultures, and the diversity into which we have all been plunged as we move closer to the millennium, that gives this place its life and its spirit. Under these conditions, at their best, we could experience the limitless variety of spiritual expression, which freedom nurtures to everyone's advantage, no matter who we are. And there is always the hope for something new, for looking ahead in confidence instead of back, dependent on the past; as Emerson assured us, "Whenever a mind is simple and receives a divine wisdom, old things pass away... it lives now, and absorbs past and future into the present hour." In this sense we are free, and it is what many have come here to find. Ralph Waldo Emerson showed us the way--he and his friends, some of whom, who knows, might have found real happiness here.

May we honor the pathways we have been given, and walk them in good company.

Resources used to prepare this sermon include Gay Wilson Allen, *Waldo Emerson* (New York: Viking Press, 1981); Ralph Waldo Emerson, "Self-Reliance," in *Basic Selections from Emerson* (New York: New American Library, 1954); Jacob Needleman, *Consciousness & Tradition* (New York: Crossroad, 1982); and *Sex, Death and God in L.A.,* ed. David Reid (New York: Pantheon, 1992).

ANY PLACE THAT IS WILD

April 27, 1997

New England Transcendentalists Ralph Waldo Emerson and Henry David Thoreau popularized nature as a spiritual reality and as a rubric for all that was wild and free. Intimacy with wilderness, however, was primarily an act of their imaginations. Thoreau's pondside cabin was only a short distance from town, where he returned regularly for hot meals and warm companions.

Emerson was a creature of the city and the village, the lecture hall, the library, and the desk. "In my study my faith is perfect," he once wrote, truthfully. From Emerson's study came images of nature in words that inspired his many readers. One of them was John Muir. He was deeply affected. Muir's reading of Emerson moved him out of his Presbyterian apostasy into the new wave of Transcendentalism. Neither were ever the same again. Transcendentalism is the "idea that the universe is permeated with the spirit of universal intelligence," a radical idea, for those who formerly sought spiritual intelligence in the Bible or the words of preachers.

For Muir, the place to seek faith was not the study, but the wilderness: "Outdoors is the place to store up spiritual influences," he wrote in one of his campfire essays. If anyone could prove it, he would. At the time he was writing about the wilderness, John Muir was the best mountaineer in the United States. An outdoorsman who could endure the harshest conditions, he experienced physical challenges as a spiritual discipline. Each vertical ascent lifted his spirit and confirmed his belief that God was in the mountains.

In endurance and in experience, Muir would surpass his intellectual mentors, Emerson and Thoreau, and transplant the Transcendental ideal to its new home in the west. John Muir surpassed his ancestry and transplanted himself as well, moving away from his family and searching for a new way to be at home in the universe.

The son of a zealot whose idea of Christian rectitude imposed exacting standards on his family, John Muir migrated as a child from

Scotland to Wisconsin, where his father pursued farming and fanaticism with equal determination. John Muir's first release from the constraints of the family took place when he entered college in Madison; several others followed.

Two years of education led him to science and naturalism; he became a teacher, briefly, and later a millworker and inventor. An industrial accident caused him to lose his sight temporarily first in one eye, then the other. When he recovered, he was a transformed person.

Life is short and hazardous, he reasoned, so he might as well set himself free to do what he wanted. "And it was from this time," he wrote, "that my long continuous wanderings may be said to have commenced. I bade adieu to all my mechanical inventions, determined to devote the rest of my life to the study of the inventions of God."

With each release from home, school, and industry, Muir's spirit turned towards the wilderness. Following a thousand-mile walk through the southeast, and a depressing stopover in New York, Muir paid forty dollars for steerage passage to California and kept going until he reached Yosemite.

Everyone who migrates to the west seeks release in one way or another. Having left home, family, years of accumulated past, we trade our roots for something new and different, something which represents freedom to us in one shape or another. For Muir, the wilderness had become his true home, first as his escape from the rigors of family life, later, as his field education in science, and ultimately, as his cultivation of the spirit.

For many of us, the journey has been similar. The West, with its open society and open spaces, has called some part of our psyche to the wilderness, where physical and spiritual challenges conjoin to produce a hardy breed of free spirits, our collective psyche a wild one. Whatever our background, the transformation we undergo as we make ourselves at home here in the west is our common defining experience. It makes us who we are.

It made Muir a tramp, a tumbleweed, a mountain man who ran from valley to peak, slept in the snow, and ate ice for breakfast. It took him years to marry and he never did settle down, becoming a benign if somewhat inattentive family man, whose house was merely a base camp, whose home was any place that was wild.

But he was gifted at more than mountaineering. His writing,

encouraged by mentors from the University of Wisconsin, prominent New York publishers, and Emerson himself, hit home with urban readers in the East. Inspired by his encounters with divinity in nature, Muir added his voice to the new Transcendentalist spirituality, giving it authenticity and an experiential quality it had lacked. That was the power in his writing.

He literally walked his talk, and no one else could keep up with him. When Ralph Waldo Emerson met John Muir in Yosemite, Emerson was already past his prime. Young Muir was disappointed that Emerson would not go camping with him, although he must have been thrilled by the recognition Emerson gave him for his literary work.

Afterwards, Muir continued to write to Emerson, begging him to return, to experience the wilderness as he had never done before. Clearly the young man would surpass the old. Emerson never did come back. I kept thinking about Emerson's missed camping opportunity as I, with my book of John Muir essays in my pack, took off one weekend last spring for my first overnight camping experience ever.

Actually it was not just one overnight; it was two, in a row. I have been preoccupied with Emerson ever since I moved west four years ago. When I lived in Emerson's New England world, attending chapel in the room where he gave his famous "Divinity School Address," even serving a church where he once was minister too, I rarely read or studied his work with personal interest. But after arriving here, I was drawn to his reflections on spirituality, nature, and the primacy of individual experience. As I trudged along the rocky path into the Joshua Tree wilderness, I identified with Emerson once again.

"Emerson never went camping," I told myself. But I did. When we push ourselves to do things we never thought we would do, we undergo transformations of who we once were, and we also become people who are different from those who went before us. Struggle and transformation cause us to evolve as individuals *and* as humankind.

There isn't any mystery why I never went camping before: as a child, I studied piano instead of joining the Girl Scouts; I had too much separation anxiety to leave my family and go to summer camp; I've never been a good sleeper, and assumed that a night outside would mean wakefulness and hypervigilant monitoring of every noise and stir.

After forty-eight years of never having done it, camping out became one of those physical and spiritual challenges destined either to defeat me or disappoint me. And I really didn't want either. And yet, one of the reasons why I moved out west was to spend more time outside in nature and less time inside my mind.

Having already undergone many day-long adventures, I knew what came next. It was time to sleep outside, to cycle from one day to another without returning to home or a hotel. Thinking about camping out has always made me feel vulnerable. Perhaps the idea of leaving home rekindled all the fears I had as a child, of getting separated from my family, fears which had been distilled, as an adult, into a dread of being uncomfortable, cold, and wet.

But transformation cannot take place unless you allow yourself to be vulnerable, to let go of assumptions about what you need to be safe and comfortable and to be yourself, and allow life to carry you through. I know all that. Still, I wasn't sure how it would go for me.

It went fine. You know, the desert sky, the comet and the stars, the warm days and cool nights, are beautiful and even I can feel at home there. But what affected me most was the awareness of how intimately related we are to the elements around us, nature, outdoors, even wilderness.

We are related in obvious ways, through the fluctuations in light and dark, hot and cold, the cycles that govern all life. We are also related in subtle, interior ways. John Muir was not so subtle in his pleading with Emerson to take a month and go camping with him in the Sierras. The experience he wanted to give him was transformation, an interior experience of change that could only happen if he were to expose himself to the elements around him.

In the study, any faith can be perfect. In the wilderness, the only faith you need is the awareness that you are part of everything you see, and affected by your exposure to it. We are as solid as rock, as fragile as flowers, as eternal as the farthest flung end of the sky. With connections like these, it's hard to stay inside your head, your study, and your outgrown ideas. Instead you are transformed by exposures of all kinds, into an altered way of being in the world.

That was the experience Muir wanted to give Emerson. He

failed there, but he surpassed the limits of his mentor. What he succeeded to do was to articulate the experience of wilderness with a passion that transformed the American view of nature itself. John Muir gave us the wilderness ideal, as a place to grow spiritually; the conservation ethic, as a responsible policy on the use of the land; and the vision of the west as a place of transformation.

Through his personal bests climbing mountains as well as his naturalist activism, we have received an image of the wilderness that we must cherish and protect for the sake of our own souls. "Outdoors is the place to store up spiritual influences," Muir wrote in what must have seemed then a radical statement about religion. Outdoors, where faith may not be perfect, it is instead a living reality in our exposure to the elements, which reminds us of who we are and what we may become if we seek our release and search any place that is wild.

Resources used to prepare this sermon include Stephen Fox, *John Muir and His Legacy: The American Conservation Movement* (Boston: Little, Brown, 1981); and *John Muir: Life and Work*, ed. Sally M. Miller (Albuquerque: University of New Mexico Press, 1993). The quotation from Ralph Waldo Emerson appears in his journals written in 1831.

LIVING WITHIN AND WITHOUT TRADITION

OUR FORGOTTEN FAITH

May 2, 1999

For three shaky years, an avant-garde magazine known as *The Dial* explored new territory in literature and religion, giving voice to radical social and spiritual views, shaking up staid Bostonians, and finally, in 1844, running out of money. The building where Ralph Waldo Emerson, Margaret Fuller, Henry David Thoreau, Bronson Alcott, and their Transcendentalist friends gathered to edit and publish their controversial journal is still standing, deep in the oldest part of downtown Boston. It's now an upscale restaurant. When I lived in Boston, I enjoyed eating there. Every time I went, I'd notice the bronze plaque commemorating *The Dial*, but like most of the patrons of the restaurant, I gave it little thought. What relevance could the visions and dreams of a small band of New England intellectuals have for the rest of us, a hundred and fifty years later?

We've moved on in so many ways. Our faith community has changed, theologically and demographically, and although we're still not as diverse as we would like to be, our religious identity has broadened and grown more inclusive. Our ideas have evolved and roamed far from our beginnings. Except for a few history buffs and people who are inexplicably drawn to the nineteenth century, we like to look ahead, not back. When we do look back, what we see is everything we've outgrown and discarded.

Living here in California, there are even fewer opportunities to be reminded of our history. Unitarian Universalism is a relatively recent arrival in the west--our church here in Santa Monica is just over seventy years old--and we have not been big players on a field already crowded with missions, new starts, revivals, native religions, and every other imaginable faith. When I landed here several years ago, it took a while for me to understand how different this spiritual landscape really is. It's invigorating, all this religious diversity, and I like it, but I've learned a couple of hard lessons from it too.

Here are some examples. At a party awhile back I was

introduced to someone who belonged to a new church with a new religion, only a couple years old. I had never heard of it, so she was eager to tell me all about it. Her religion was based on the teachings of Ralph Waldo Emerson, she told me. "Really?" I responded, incredulously. "So is ours." I came away feeling slightly affronted by the fact that another group had claimed one of our gods for their own. They didn't even know he was one of ours.

Another example: some time ago I took part in a series of interfaith meetings in which the members were all invited to present their faith tradition and religious beliefs. Everyone except me, that is. Apparently everyone assumed that Unitarian Universalists have no tradition of our own, but just believe a little bit of everyone else's, so there was no need for me to add anything at all.

Our appetite for learning about world religions, our comfort with our own theological diversity, and our reluctance to frighten or worse, bore people by talking about ourselves, are virtues. At best we are so comfortable with who we are that we do not feel pressed for self-definition. We are grounded in principles that feel like second nature to us, so we act on them, rather than explain them. No wonder that people viewing us from outside our community tend to see us as adventurous and untroubled, celebrating every holiday on the calendar, believing whatever we choose. Our openness is a strength. But it gives a diffuse character to our faith, misleading others and sometimes even ourselves. Some see our openness as an absence of conviction, lending our dilettantish enthusiasms an increasingly shorter attention span, jumping from one thing to another, standing for nothing. Some of us enjoy the exposure to different ideas and approaches, never realizing that all the ways we are--open and free, inclusive and adventurous, diverse and fun-loving--are exactly what our predecessors hoped we would one day become.

To understand, practice, and represent our faith we need to know our history. That is especially true for us since we are always growing and changing. Without our past, we lose the thread of connection to the tradition that *makes* us open and free. We fail to see that our tradition has given us the durable and trustworthy faith we have today, a set of spiritual and social values that we believe makes us better people.

A couple of weeks ago I sat in a UCLA library reading

unpublished microfilm pages from *The Dial*. I was there because I've read excerpts from that short-lived journal in anthologies of Emerson and Thoreau, and I wanted to know more. One excerpt, an essay by Emerson on the Hindu scriptures the Vedas, was evidence that the Transcendentalists were interested in Eastern religions. I developed an image of Ralph Waldo Emerson as a nineteenth-century Ram Dass, way ahead of his time.

Reading *The Dial*, I scored a big discovery. Emerson did write about the Vedas in *The Dial*, and Henry David Thoreau wrote about Zoroaster and the Chinese philosopher Mencius. They were part of a series of articles titled "The Ethical Scriptures," essays on non-biblical writings.

In the introduction, the editor writes, "Each nation has its Bible more or less pure; none has yet been willing or able in a wise and devout spirit to collate its own with those of other nations." The editor-- either Margaret Fuller or Emerson--goes on to hope that some day we will "bring together the grand expressions of the moral sentiment of different ages and races, the rules for guidance of life, the bursts of piety and of abandonment to the Invisible and Eternal;--a work which we hope to be done by religion." Our proclivity for religious variety-- east and west--springs from this early impulse to make a tapestry, a perennial philosophy, out of all that is good and wise in the human narrative of faith. When we turn to Zen Buddhism or Christian contemplative prayer, to labyrinths or sweat lodges, we are practicing our spiritual discipline, to be curators of all that is precious, applicable, and lively in the world of religion: to seek "the Invisible and the Eternal" by embracing an ever-widening spectrum of possibilities; which, when you think about eternity, is a very smart thing to do.

To be Unitarian Universalist is to belong to a community of open-minded people who believe that inspiration and direction can be found in any worthy pursuit and sincere quest for insight. When Emerson and Thoreau were busy writing about "ethical scriptures" for *The Dial*, Unitarianism was still very young, the new liberal religion as their mentor Channing defined it. In this sense you could say that our interest in world religions has been with us from the beginning. Those of you who have found spiritual direction from Buddhist teachings, or pagan ritual, or Jewish meditation are not defecting from our faith, you are practicing it.

We don't all have to practice it that way, however. In a wonderful essay titled "Why I Don't Meditate," Anne Lamott confesses, "I have been reading books on meditation with great enthusiasm since 1975, but have not quite gotten around to becoming a person who meditates." These days she remains "utterly committed" to the "idea of meditating," though what she actually finds herself doing is praying "like a mother, in the mo-fo sense of the word." Though I do know Unitarian Universalists who meditate and practice a spiritual discipline with regularity, I know a lot more like Anne Lamott. Or people like me who try to get away with claiming our workouts as a spiritual discipline.

Not to worry: the Transcendentalist heritage offers other paths as well. William Ellery Channing mentioned them in the reading for the morning: his "two noble places of study," the library and the beach. None of our options is exclusive. Our heritage teaches us that when it comes to religious wisdom, inclusive is always better than exclusive. Search as far and wide as you can, draw from the inner world and the outer reaches of human experience. You will learn and grow, as Channing wrote, in the company of the "great and the beautiful."

The spiritual and social value that runs through our tradition is the idea that we can shape ourselves, through learning and reflection, into good people, "great and beautiful" people, even. This powerfully optimistic point of view came from the Transcendentalists, in their confidence in human intuition, in the individual capacity to discover truth for ourselves. This capacity never abandons us. It has a life of its own that is independent of all outside influences, religious or otherwise. Trust in it and you will find your way.

In the beginning of his essay "Self-Reliance," Emerson writes, "To believe your own thought, to believe that what is true for you in your private heart is true for all…that is genius." That affirmation remains the center of our faith. That is the thread that runs from the past to the present, and connects one person to another, in this community of seekers we call our church.

Some people have blamed Emerson's philosophy, with its emphasis on self-trust and intuition, for the less appealing aspects of individualism that are part of the American ethos--its self-absorption and materialism. But they have overlooked the undercurrent of social conscience that is implicit in Emerson's work. Emerson and the Transcendentalists were active social reformers, throwing themselves into the abolition movement, forming utopian communes, and learning civil disobedience. Transcendentalism is an imaginative and spiritual elaboration of the simple moral law, Kant's categorical imperative: act according to an ethic that can be applied to all, the "golden rule." The liberating influence of Transcendentalism is pervasive. When Mahatma Gandhi turned to Thoreau's essay on "Civil Disobedience" in preparation for leading his people to freedom, he "was only taking back what Thoreau himself had ... learned from ... India." The lessons of those "ethical scriptures" that Emerson and Thoreau had published in *The Dial* had far-reaching social and moral consequences that cut back and forth across old boundaries. They prove that every step we take towards widening our horizons, opening our minds, and acting from our hearts, leads not just ourselves, but all people, towards "the great and the beautiful."

They surface in acts of conscience and service, in love of learning, and in reverence for the earth. They are everywhere we are, living our faith just as our predecessors hoped we would: open and free, eccentric, but not without charm (we hope), one in our humanity and connected by the thread of truth into a great tapestry of faith.

Resources used to prepare this sermon include Anne Lamott, "Why I Don't Meditate" in *The Best Spiritual Writing,* ed. Philip Zaleski (San Francisco: Harper, 1998); William Ellery Channing, "Self-Culture" in *The Works of William Ellery Channing, D.D.* (Boston: American Unitarian Association, 1875); Robert D. Richardson, Jr., "The Social Imperatives of Transcendentalism" in *Religious Humanism* (Spring 1988); "The Ethical Scriptures," a series in *The Dial* (Boston, 1842-1844); and the writings of Ralph Waldo Emerson. The quotation from Gandhi appears in Robert D. Richardson, Jr., "The Social Imperatives of Transcendentalism," *Religious Humanism* (Spring 1988).

A ROMANTIC WOMAN

May 9, 1999

Sometimes when I look back on my life, I see all the people I never actually met, who kept me company in my mind. Like a room full of imaginary playmates, they add a dimension of experience that has its own reality and meaning. They belong to memories of where I lived, and of what I was doing, and just like friends and family, they were there too. Sometimes I talk about them: Aldous Huxley, William and Alice James, Ralph Waldo Emerson, Eleanor Roosevelt. Their life stories express values and struggles that touch me with their integrity, originality and strength.

In her new book *Winter Hours,* Mary Oliver invokes the names of her "great ones," as she calls her imaginary companions. She remembers them as "Forebears, models, spirits whose influence and teachings I am now inseparable from, and forever grateful for. I go nowhere, I arrive nowhere, without them," she writes. "With them I live my life, with them I enter the event, I mold the meditation, I keep if I can some essence of the hour, even as it slips away. And I do not accomplish this alert and loving confrontation by myself and alone," she adds, "but through terrifying and continual effort, and with this innumerable, fortifying company, bright as stars in the heaven of my mind."

One of the newer, brighter stars to occupy my mind is Margaret Fuller, nineteenth-century writer and feminist, Transcendentalist cohort, nominal Unitarian. Until recently I knew very little about her. What I did know were fragments of the stories some told, conveying ridicule and contempt. She frightened people. Even her friends-- Emerson, and two others--did her a tremendous disservice when shortly after she died, they assembled her memoirs. These "memoirs" were a fictionalized account of her life, little more than a spin job to give her a more conventional legacy than the real one. The real one was far more interesting. Historians today view Margaret Fuller with greater understanding and appreciation. That makes sense; she was way ahead of her time. One of her admirers, Henry Wadsworth Longfellow, commented that "it is easy enough now to say and see what she then saw and said, but it demanded insight to see and courage to say what was entirely missed by [her] generation."

That is tragic, and much of Margaret Fuller's life was tragic. Yet her raw courage and emotional honesty transformed her tragic life into a heroic one. For all its anguish and struggle, and perhaps because of it--her story is inspiring and highly instructive.

At first glimpse, you might only see a life that is doomed to disappointment. A smart daughter raised by a father who wished his first born had been a boy, she received the education a young man would receive. Unfortunately for Margaret, that meant she could never leave home, since there were no schools for girls offering her an education equivalent to Harvard, where the men in her family went to school. Siblings were born, some died, Margaret stayed home and took care of them. When her father died, she took responsibility for supporting the entire family, working as a tutor and a teacher.

Through her teaching connections, she met Ralph Waldo Emerson. Her intellect and conversational wit impressed him. They collaborated on *The Dial*, the Transcendentalist magazine. As editor, Margaret never earned a penny.

During *The Dial* years, Margaret began a series of conversations for women, recruiting the wives of her Transcendentalist friends as participants. Together they created an environment in a Boston parlor that was as stimulating as a Harvard classroom, probably more so. In these meetings, Margaret developed her technique as a literary critic, exchanged views on the arts with other self-educated women, and became a feminist.

She left *The Dial*. She went west--as far as Wisconsin. Her essay about her visit there, social criticism disguised as a travelogue, revealed her concern for the plight of Native Americans, slaves, and women. Universalist publisher Horace Greeley liked her writing and hired her to work for the *New York Tribune*. She went to New York, lived alone, hoped a romance would flourish; it didn't. She went to Europe. From there she sent back dispatches and the *Tribune* paid her for them. This way she eked by as the first American woman to make a living as a journalist.

At the age of thirty-six, free of family responsibilities at last, she traveled throughout Europe and settled in Italy. She met an impoverished Italian nobleman who was involved in the cause to win Italy's independence. Margaret joined him in the movement. They had a child together.

Desperately poor, hoping to return to America so that Margaret could publish the history of Italy she had written while living in Rome, they boarded the cheapest passage they could find, and set sail. The ship's captain died, and the poorly made vessel, ineptly steered and buffeted by a hurricane, sank within sight of Fire Island, New York. Margaret Fuller, her partner Giovanni Ossoli, and her son Angelo, all drowned. Margaret Fuller was forty years old. Her trunk full of manuscripts was never recovered.

Much was lost in Margaret Fuller's life, but even more was gained, which is why her example is so compelling to me. She lived by dint of determination and honesty, and the sum of the effort is something to admire. Though she was deprived of the encouragement and the acceptance she deserved, nothing squelched her inner will. She surpassed the limitations others placed on her. She handled dreary teaching assignments--which she loathed--by taking time to write, to study, to improve her own mind. She never accepted her lot, no matter how many times it was handed to her. She chose instead to trust her ambition, to speak her mind, whatever the social costs, to become known as a writer and to dream of being the beloved partner of a man who would value her for who she was. She was often disappointed. But she never gave up.

Her writing, while not at all self-pitying, expressed her yearning for love. Yet she learned through several unrequited romances that the men who enjoyed her as an intellectual equal had no desire for her as a mate. She wrote about power, about the inner drive to be "brought out towards perfection," and her longing for self-actualization. Yet many in her circle disapproved of her stridency, and her insistence on being heard.

Her book, *Woman in the Nineteenth Century*, was controversial in many respects. As a platform for social reform, it took on unpopular causes, advocating for women prostitutes and prisoners. But even more radical was her suggestion that women deserved an education comparable to men, because women were beings "of infinite scope," comparable to men. Margaret Fuller's feminist ideas no longer sound radical to us. Her friends were probably not shocked by them either. Margaret Fuller shocked people by daring to live by her ideas, not settling for talking about them, but rather by living as if she were a being of "infinite scope" too.

Margaret Fuller did not come into her own until she left the rarefied atmosphere of Transcendentalist New England, moving first to New York and then to Europe. These departures were defining pathways for her. In the working world of New York and the political ferment of Italy, she moved freely and effectively, on her own. It couldn't have been easy--she was independent, but lonely; gainfully employed but impoverished; yet she did it anyway. Margaret Fuller strained hard against the limits some set on her, yet in that struggle, she won what she so fervently hoped to have: a writing career, a partner and child, a romantic life. Though she also lost it early, she never would have found it at all by playing it safe, staying in place.

Margaret Fuller was a romantic in the sense that she believed in her striving and trusted where it would lead. Her close identification with oppressed people, whether they were women prisoners, Native Americans living on a reservation, African-American slaves, or Italian revolutionaries, shows that her heart was in the human struggle for freedom. The struggle was costly; she saw how some lost everything they had. But whatever the sacrifice, the ideal would always triumph and nothing was ever lost in the end.

Margaret Fuller was a woman who let her true self lead her life, who refused to be meek and knew she would never be popular, yet still dared to hope that she would find what she really wanted. She was vulnerable and transparent, smart enough to know it, honest enough not to hide who she was. It must have hurt--a lot--to be this way. She was brave enough not to let that stop her.

What I admire about Margaret Fuller is the combination of idealism, honesty and vulnerability that shaped her lasting character. She represents the woman who pushes herself just a little further than is comfortable--for herself and for others--and makes the world more open to those who come after her.

Everything I have ever done that really meant something to me came from being honest with myself and risking whatever was at stake to live by that truth. I've done that a few times; so have you. Margaret Fuller did it over and over again, until her life assumed the heroic sheen that comes from long exposure to truth and to risk. Her true self survives all hurt, all disappointment, all fear, and though her life may have been lost long ago, her true self is still good company--fortifying and exhorting every one of us: to your self be true too.

Resources used to prepare this sermon include Mary Oliver, *Winter Hours: Prose, Prose Poems, and Poems* (New York: Houghton Mifflin, 1999).

A TRUTH OF ONE'S OWN

October 13, 1996

In the classic narrative *Autobiography of a Yogi,* the story of Paramahansa Yogananda, Hindu swami and founder of the Self-Realization Fellowship, you can find, amid the mysterious events, teachings, and travels of a yogi's life, a most interesting account of his meeting with the Unitarians. For it was at their invitation that Swami Yogananda addressed the International Congress of Religious Liberals, which gathered in Boston in October, 1920. A photograph of the event shows the robed Swami surrounded by Unitarians, serious-looking men in starched collars. The contrast and formality, however, convey nothing but mutual respect and sincere hospitality.

Yogananda was apprehensive about addressing the meeting. He feared that his grasp of English was inadequate to convey his message. Yet he rose magnificently to the occasion, and his first address to American citizens was noted by the secretary of the American Unitarian Association in the published account of the proceedings: Swami Yogananda, it said, delegate from the Brahmacharya Ashram of Ranchi, brought the greetings of his Association to the Congress.

In fluent English and with a forceful delivery he gave an address of a philosophical character on "The Science of Religion," which has been printed in pamphlet form for a wider distribution. Religion, he maintained, is universal and it is one. We cannot possibly universalize particular customs and conventions; but the common element in religion can be universalized, and we may ask all alike to follow and obey it.

This historic meeting was only one of several the Unitarians had convened since 1893. Excited by the possibilities of interfaith dialogue, fascinated by the spiritual practices of Eastern religions, and energized by their curiosity, Unitarians met more than one boat at the Boston docks, welcoming foreign visitors. The Unitarian relationship with India is itself historic. Initially intent on founding Unitarian groups there, our missionaries forged alliances instead with liberal

Hindus. One alliance, which Unitarian Jabez Sunderland initiated with the liberal Hindu group Brahmo Samaj, continues to this day. Jabez Sunderland is one of the starch-collared Unitarians shown in the picture with Swami Yogananda.

The interest and curiosity Unitarians have maintained about other religions began early, with the spiritual search of Ralph Waldo Emerson and his Transcendentalist peers. Emerson's appreciation of Hinduism evolved slowly. Initially he viewed Indian religion as nothing more than superstition. But his reading of European philosophers led him to a much more sophisticated understanding of Hindu scripture, which he read with interest and respect. As Emerson's biographer, Robert D. Richardson, Jr., writes, Emerson understood that here in the *Bhagavad Gita* was a belief in the fundamental identity of all things, beyond and beneath appearances, and a profound conception of universal justice and equilibrium. Emerson's encounter with Eastern religion was fateful. Moving beyond his own cultural and religious assumptions, he moved Unitarianism from liberal Christianity to spiritual diversity.

Unitarian Universalism today includes an appreciation of the scripture and practices of other religions. The banners on our sanctuary wall vividly convey our affirmation of the co-equal prominence of the major world religions. Many members of this congregation include Buddhist meditation, or Jewish cultural celebrations, or Hindu worship at the Self-Realization Fellowship in their spiritual lives.

Openness and curiosity have traveled with us on our religious journey. And like goodness and mercy, I hope they will follow us all the days of our lives.

The spiritual search we have conducted for the past hundred and fifty years, however, has not always illuminated our own tradition as well as it has educated us about others. Contemporary Unitarian Universalists often express confusion about what it is that our faith really has to say. It is easier to point the way to some other faith, which may be less reluctant to declare itself. Such a tentative approach to our own tradition may produce a diverse and uncritical community, but it also deprives us of the grounding we really need.

Some have mistakenly assumed that Unitarian Universalism is a syncretistic religion, standing for nothing on its own, assimilating whatever feels right at the time. They leave as easily as they enter, in search of something more sustaining than they have taken from their sojourn with us. We fail these people, and each other, when we fail to credit our own tradition for the affirmations and tools of our spiritual life. We have them, and we do not know it. These affirmations and tools are the instincts that led Emerson out of the ideological constraints of the Unitarianism of his time, and into Transcendentalism, which has given us the Unitarianism of our time.

They are the principles that gave Boston's Unitarians the momentum to launch an interfaith movement that brought Indian religion to this country. They are the truth and the way of our own faith, and in it are the affirmations and tools of the spiritual life we seek. Through it we become more truly ourselves, which is the goal of all religions, whatever the path they take.

To find your own truth, you must take your own path. A couple of years ago, the Dalai Lama addressed a Christian audience by offering a commentary on the Gospels. This historic occasion has recently been reported by Robert Kiely, in a book titled *The Good Heart: A Buddhist Perspective on the Teachings of Jesus.* The Dalai Lama's approach is one we can appreciate. Demonstrating scholarship, modesty, and respect for a faith he does not embrace himself, the Dalai Lama presented a Buddhist reading of the Christian Gospels.

He proved that religious traditions are not diminished by investigation by outsiders. He also affirmed the integrity of diverse approaches to truth. Kiely writes, "From the outset, [the Dalai Lama] gently and quietly reassured his listeners that the last thing he had come to do was 'sow seeds of doubt' among Christians about their own faith." Again and again, he counseled people to deepen their understanding and appreciation of their own traditions, pointing out that human sensibilities and cultures are too varied to justify a single "way" to the Truth. He gently, but firmly and repeatedly, resisted suggestions that Buddhism and Christianity are different languages for the same essential beliefs. He cautioned against people calling themselves "Buddhist-Christians," just as one should not try, (as he warns), "to put a yak's head on a sheep's body."

It is this sensitivity that we Unitarian Universalists share. Recognizing that many faiths, especially Christianity, require a fervent loyalty to one and only one path, we have chosen instead the way of diversity and openness. We do not attempt to reconcile fundamentally different views, by putting on yaks' heads and looking ridiculous. Rather, aware that one of the spiritual practices of our Unitarian Universalist faith is the deep and responsible engagement with other religions, we study--beginning with what we teach our youngest children--how to approach them. Like the Dalai Lama, who is certainly a good role model, it is our intention to approach other faiths with modesty and respect.

Perhaps it is a subtle distinction I am making here, but it is an important one all the same. To be a Unitarian Universalist is to seek and to enjoy the wisdom of what we learn from others, and to become our own true selves. The integrity of our investigation resides in the fact that we assume no superior knowledge or desire to convert others; on the contrary, we believe that to *learn* is to grow spiritually. This conviction can also be applied to the reality of global interdependence; as Diana Eck writes, "The world is not yet interrelated in the sense of actively and intentionally creating the international, intercultural, and interreligious relationships that will sustain a world in which we depend upon one another as much as we do."

From Emerson's transformative reading of the *Bhagavad Gita* to the unlikely advocacy by the Boston Brahmins for Hindu swamis and other representatives of the non-Christian world, we have demonstrated that we can only be improved by the openness we bring to such encounters.

What we do with what we learn is another challenge as well. This is where our own spiritual practices and perspectives can help us, and why we need to know what they are. In a paper entitled "The Roots of Spirituality: Self-Culture in New England Transcendentalism," Unitarian Universalist historian David Robinson notes, "For the Unitarians [in the time of William Ellery Channing--mid-nineteenth century], life was best thought of as a dynamic process, a continuing spiritual growth or development." Channing explained the organic analogy that underlay their conception: "To cultivate any thing, be it a plant, an animal, a mind, is to make grow. Growth, expansion is the end." The Unitarians thus reformulated the spiritual life as a process of growth, improvement, and the nurturing cultivation of the spiritual potential of every self. So much of what we think is new, such as the yearning for spiritual growth expressed by so many of you, has been part of our tradition as long as we have called ourselves "Unitarians."

To learn and to grow *is* the life of the spirit for us.

There is another aspect of our tradition, a theological affirmation, that may also help us to appreciate the way in which our tradition has nurtured us without our even knowing it. It is not unique, but it is as much a part of who we are as it was of Swami Yogananda, who said, in his address to the International Congress of Religious Liberals, that religion is universal and it is one.

It is also expressed in the Sikh words with which I opened the service: "As fragrance dwells in a flower, or reflection in a mirror, so the Divine dwells inside everything; seek therefore in your own heart." There is ample evidence of this insight in many other faiths as well: the Hindu priest teaches his son that growth comes from something we cannot see, the inside of a fig seed; he says, "The invisible everywhere in the world is the spirit in the world." We believe this too. We believe that inside each of us there is a divine seed, a holy center, a spark of life, a sense of truth, that gives each of us, no matter who we are, no matter what our abilities or opportunities, equal access to the spirit. We maintain a radical affirmation of the human potential to experience the holy, to grow and to give substantively to the world, and to make it better.

That is what we believe. It comes from William Ellery Channing, and his investigation of self-culture. It comes from Ralph Waldo Emerson, and his immortal pronouncement in the essay "Self-Reliance": "Nothing is at last sacred but the integrity of your own mind." You, whoever you are, have a truth of your own. And that truth, when it comes to religion, points to the faith that goes beyond all specific traditions. It points to the universal, the individual truth that is shared, at its depths, with all people, the qualities and the values that transcend all narrow affiliations and identities.

Difficult to express and even harder to organize, this free spirit is the core of our faith. It is the journey, the song of life, the wisdom we seek and often find when we open ourselves to the world and its variety. It is the truth that leads us to our true selves. With the affirmations of our faith, may we keep to our path, seeking always to learn, to grow, and to experience the holy in our own way. This life is ours for that purpose. May we make it so.

Resources used to prepare this sermon include Diana Eck, *Encountering God: A Spiritual Journey from Bozeman to Banaras* (Boston: Beacon Press, 1993); Ralph Waldo Emerson, "Self-Reliance" in *Selections from Ralph Waldo Emerson*, ed. Stephen E. Whicher (Boston: Houghton Mifflin, 1960); Paramahansa Yogananda, *Autobiography of a Yogi* (Los Angeles: Self Realization Fellowship, 1993); Robert Kiely, preface in His Holiness the Dalai Lama, *The Good Heart: A Buddhist Perspective on the Teachings of Jesus* (Boston: Wisdom Publications, 1996); Spencer Lavan, *Unitarians and India* (Chicago: Exploration Press, 1991); Roy D. Phillips, *Transforming Liberal Congregations for the New Millennium* (St. Paul: Unity Church, 1996); and Robert D. Richardson, Jr., *Emerson: The Mind on Fire* (Berkeley: University of California Press, 1995).

DOWN TO EARTH

January 28, 1996

For one week in June, in a different place in the U.S. or Canada each year, Unitarian Universalists gather for the meeting of our continental religious community. Last year, delegates to the General Assembly in Spokane, Washington, debated--not for the first time--who we were and where we had come from. Identity can be a consuming issue for Unitarian Universalists. If you celebrate individualism and practice democracy, you'll have to take a vote every time you want to declare your convictions as a group.

So it was no small achievement that the group voted to add a new affirmation to its list of "Principles and Purposes," the statement of our convictions we adopted over ten years ago. The "Principles and Purposes" statement affirms the core values of our movement. It describes our faith as a "living tradition," evolving out of a variety of sources. These sources are familiar to many of us: the Jewish and Christian teachings; the wisdom of the world religions; humanist counsel to heed reason and the results of science; the words and deeds of prophetic men and women who call us to the cause of justice and compassion; and the direct experience of the holy, in the spirit of the Transcendentalists and expressed in all cultures.

Onto this expansive backdrop for our contemporary living faith, we have added one more source: "Spiritual teachings of earth-centered traditions which celebrate the sacred circle of life and instruct us to live in harmony with the rhythms of nature." This "sixth source," as insiders like to call it, was predictably controversial: how ready are we for the inclusion of pagan practices and native cultures? How authentic can we be in appropriating their wisdom? What can we take to use with respect and decency, and what is opportunistic adventuring in worlds we have already conquered? Optimism prevailed. We adopted the amendment, validating our interest in earth-centered spirituality and all that may come of it. The vote lends institutional recognition to initiatives such as the Covenant of Unitarian Universalist Pagans--CUUPS--we have a chapter here; and the incorporation of native religions and their teachings into our own. Well, we were doing it anyway. True to its purposes, the democratic process affirmed who we already were.

Now comes the time to explore what it means. To live in harmony with the rhythms of nature is an ambitious goal for most of us. Since I've moved to Los Angeles, I've had to accept that I must live in harmony with the rhythms of fluctuating air quality--and the sinus problems they impose. Beyond that, nature is a vast and somewhat impersonal reality. I am a limited outdoor activities enthusiast, rarely doing more than the occasional day hike or trip to take in the visual beauty of our surroundings. But it's not just me. It's difficult for most of us to describe how to have a relationship with nature. Even Black Elk wrote, "Then I was standing on the highest mountain of them all, and round beneath me was the whole hoop of the world. And while I stood there I saw more than I can tell and I understood more than I saw." Our comprehension of nature is both intuitive and inarticulate.

That is why I turn to the writings of Edward O. Wilson, evolutionary biologist, when I want to understand how to approach nature. As he declared in his exploration of life's affinity for life, a tendency called "biophilia," instinct is in this rare instance aligned with reason. Our instinctive love of nature makes sense. It makes sense because evolution demands a conservation ethic for survival, and also because, as Wilson himself says, "our spirit is woven from it, hope rises on its currents."

Wilson is an interesting character. A lifelong explorer naturalist, he built a career in evolutionary biology that has yielded several acclaimed books, including the ever popular *Insect Societies,* and the controversial *Sociobiology* and *On Human Nature.* Shunned by molecular biologists for his steadfast pursuit of discovering and inventorying new species of ants, vilified by colleagues who found his sociobiology theory politically repugnant, Wilson has accumulated his share of critics. Theologians argue against Wilson's extending his biological view to human nature itself, offended by his contention that human beings evolved from apes. Given the storm of protest *Sociobiology* stirred up, even Wilson reflected in his memoir, "Perhaps I should have stopped at chimpanzees when I wrote the book." Nevertheless he remains one of my great heroes. Reading his books has helped me to understand and to appreciate the spiritual dimension of our affinity for life and its mysteries. He combines instinct and reason with the humility one acquires from a genuine relationship with nature. He has it.

How he got it is a story worth reading. In *Naturalist*, Wilson's memoir, he writes about his early enthusiasm for the creatures of the Alabama swamps not far from his family home. By the time he was fifteen, he not only knew all about the native flora and fauna, he interacted with them with ease. "A swamp filled with snakes may be a nightmare to most," Wilson writes, "but for me it was a ceaselessly rotating lattice of wonders. I had the same interest in the diversity of snakes that other fifteen-year-old boys seemed automatically to develop in the years and makes of automobiles. And knowing them well, I had no fear." But that fearless adolescent spirit eventually brought him trouble. While serving as a nature counselor at Boy Scout Camp Pushmataha, Wilson survived a bite inflicted by a pygmy rattlesnake, an unfortunate and painful moment of hubris he was nevertheless inclined to repeat. Once, he arm-wrestled a cottonmouth so large it could easily have killed him. Looking back from the age of sixty-six, Wilson's recollection of the episode reveals some deeper wisdom:

> This narrow escape was the most adrenaline-charged moment of my year's adventures.... Since then I have cast back, trying to retrieve my emotions to understand why I explored swamps and hunted snakes with such dedication and recklessness. The activities gave me little or no heightened status among my peers; I never told anyone most of what I did....My reasons were mixed. They were partly exhilaration at my entry into a beautiful and complex new world. And partly possessiveness; I had a place that no one else knew. And vanity; I believed that no one, anywhere, was better at exploring woods and finding snakes. And ambition; I dreamed I was training myself someday to be a professional field biologist. And finally, an undeciphered residue, a yearning remaining deep within me that I have never understood, nor wish to, for fear that if named it might vanish.

"While I stood there, I saw more than I can tell and I understood more than I saw." This love of nature, the undecipherable residue of evolution, forms our identity as definitively as the artifacts of humanity's feverish efforts to build a civilization. Our sixth spiritual source goes deeper than earth-centered traditions: it goes straight to the earth itself.

We are urban people, most of us. Few of us have been arm-wrestling rattlesnakes in the Los Angeles canyons lately. Some of us have been reading *The Wall Street Journal*, however, and noted what appeared, rather incongruously, on its pages this week: an essay titled "The Spirit in Technology," by San Francisco Bay area writer Tom Mahon. He describes the way in which technology has imposed a disconnection between the physical landscape and the moral one, resulting in a lamentable loss of spiritual life in contemporary society. If you seek a spiritual life, he suggests, reconnect the physical and the moral landscape. He writes, "The great naturalist John Muir once said, 'I find that if I touch anything, it's connected to everything else in the universe.'" True spirituality is an exquisite awareness of the interconnections of all things. Even *The Wall Street Journal* and nature itself.

You don't need to be a John Muir or an Edward O. Wilson to know that life affiliates with life, is endlessly fascinated with its creatures, its spaces, its connections of rhythm and harmony as they are experienced each day. The instinct is part of our nature. Our existence depends on it; our spirit is woven from it, hope rises on its currents. Don't like snakes? Even Wilson, who climbed to an elevation of 13,000 feet, gasping for breath, pushing his physical limit, in search of an undiscovered species of ant, admits he is afraid of spiders.

What matters is any way the connection takes place for you. The sun on your head through the sunroof of your car, the ritual observance of the solstice, the sight of the stars in the desert sky at night--the possibilities for connection are endless and awe-inspiring. Make the effort to combine wonder and reason and you too, like Wilson and Muir, will become advocates for conservation and biodiversity.

Wilson, the explorer naturalist, still fantasizes about an unexplored and endless new world. The great majority of species of organisms--possibly in excess of ninety percent--remain unknown to science. Earth, in the dazzling variety of its life, is still a little-known planet. And so is our ever-expanding universe in space, as seen through the Hubble telescope. The more you look, you see more than you can tell, and understand more than you can see.

When I think about all the things in life I cannot understand, suffering and injustice, as they have inscribed themselves on human history, and the fears I bear from one day to the next, there are only so many comforting places to turn. To other people, of course, and to the loving connections that keep us whole. And to nature, whatever sense of nature I have fashioned out of my limited exposure and urban adventures, but still nature and still there to remind me of my own tiny but very real place in the universe. A creature of this earth, I belong to something far greater than I can see or know, and yet when I look, I know more than I can say. That is a spiritual life, or the beginning of one. And it is a beginning that each of us can find. No matter where we have come from, or what has influenced us, we all came from mother earth, where, when it all comes down, as the blues song says, we all got to go back.

Perhaps that is all we need to know. To know we belong to the earth, to protect the earth and its creatures, to take the earth's wisdom into ourselves, to trust the instinct and to heed the reason that tells us this is all we have and it is more than enough--from this knowing, comes our spirit and our hope. May we live as if life itself depends on it.

Resources used to prepare this sermon include Edward O. Wilson, *Biophilia* (Harvard University Press, 1984) and *Naturalist* (New York: Warner Books, 1995); Black Elk, "The Sacred Hoop" (No. 614) and "Principles and Purposes" in *Singing the Living Tradition* (Boston: Beacon Press, 1993). Thanks to Fran Hotchkiss for calling my attention to Tom Mahon's "The Spirit in Technology" in *The Wall Street Journal* January 12, 1996.

FAITH TRANSFORMATIONS

May 5, 1996

Nowadays--and nobody knows this better than we do--you can choose your religion the same way you can demonstrate brand loyalty at the supermarket. Stunning conversions have always added something extra to the religious landscape, however, and we are familiar with the lore of dramatic transformations: Saul of Tarsus, converted on the roadside; Thomas Merton, plucked from profligacy; even the Buddha, enlightened by the spectacle of suffering. Today, religious conversion still possesses drama and intensity, even if such choices acquire increasing similarity with other kinds of consumerism in the marketplace of life. Perhaps the drama and intensity are part of the appeal, so great is our desire for ultimacy and meaning. That would explain why a recent study reveals that about thirty percent of Americans will switch religious affiliations in their lifetimes. It's part of our cultural heritage.

According to *New York Times* writer Stephen J. Dubner, "This is a particularly American opportunity and one that is being exploited in ever-increasing numbers. To be convinced, you only need to stick your head into an overflowing Catholic conversion workshop, a mosque filled with American-born blacks, a 5,000-member 'megachurch' that caters to forward-looking Protestants or a tiny Pentecostal church packed with Hispanic immigrants who came here as Catholics."

And then there's us. We must have twice as many converts as the national average, with members coming into our fellowship from backgrounds as diverse as the demographics of our metropolitan area. Not that we tend to see ourselves as converts in the traditional sense, and not that we are. For many of us, coming in to this community does not require rejecting the religion of our childhood. Rather, the choice involves a culling of what we carry with us, some of it to be discarded, the rest to be tenderly revisited when the time is right.

But we, too, are riding the wave of religious choice. "By now," Dubner writes, "choosing a religion is no longer a novel idea. Ours is an era marked by the desire to define--or redefine--ourselves. We have been steadily remaking ourselves along ethnic, political, sexual, linguistic, and cultural lines, carefully sewing new stripes into our personal flags and waving them with vigor."

Some parents now raise their children, anticipating that they will make an individual religious choice when they come of age. I remember being shocked when I heard someone say, "I'm raising my children as Episcopalians, so when they rebel, they'll be rebelling against a proper, elegant religion." It seemed so cynical to me, to expose one's offspring to religious faith as if it were merely a museum full of old masters, with which every educated person should be familiar. At its lowest point, such religion offers an identity, such as Christian, with all of its conventions and none of its faith.

That may well be why people do move on to find something new. Religious search is a fiercely personal quest, with questions of life and death and ultimacy and meaning hanging in the balance. People who go to the trouble of converting are seeking to express their newfound identity with their whole selves. They bring a fervor to their practice that strengthens the self-made destiny their choice has given them.

To choose a new religion is to bring a degree of intentionality and need to the choice that is very different from the practice of childhood faith. Stephen J. Dubner, writing his own story of conversion in *The New York Times*, describes an unusual family history. His parents, both Jews, each converted to Catholicism. They met at a Catholic church, fell in love, married, had eight children, and lived the rest of their lives as ardent Catholics. Dubner, recalling his parents' choice to renounce Judaism and embrace Christianity, contrasts their needs with his, which led him to convert back to Judaism. "It left us wanting different things," he says. "My mother, recognizing life's temporality, was determined to insure a life everlasting. For reasons I can't explain, I was less consumed with beating back the darkness of death than with finding a schematic for the here and now. A schematic, which included study of the Torah, immersion in Jewish customs and dating Jewish women, also provided an identity." While Dubner's parents seem to have been searching for a religious faith, what their son needed was something else--a reappropriation of who he was, in religious terms. Fair enough, to want identity as well as faith, from your religion.

These struggles are familiar to many of us. I can remember how many years I questioned my religious identity, even before I needed any kind of faith. My father, who had been raised as a secular Jew, and my mother, the product of a Protestant-Catholic intermarriage, were all too familiar with the constraints imposed by religious identity. Seeking a broader and more tolerant religious environment, they made the move into Unitarian Universalism comfortably and happily. Religious humanists, they were ready to shed their childhood faith and to affiliate with others who felt the same way.

For my parents' children, conscious of our religious roots, the question of identity could not be resolved so decisively. We inherited the Unitarian Universalist faith, which is a perspective, not an identity, and which left us to resolve what our identity would be. In my adolescent years, I debated endlessly about it. I still do, in some ways. I do not feel like I belong--nor do I share the beliefs--of either Christian or Jewish communities, and am uncomfortable when either group asserts its distinctive mission or tribal claims. The discomfort, I must be the first to admit, reflects my feeling that I have no such claims to make for myself. I know that I will never identify with Christianity or Judaism, one or the other. And my Unitarian Universalist perspective, while I embrace it fully and give it my complete loyalty, does not give me an identity in the same way a Christian or a Jew has one. Now I have come to realize that it is not supposed to.

In the past few years, I have moved along in my own religious journey, pushed past the struggle over identity--a push I needed, because I was so enmeshed in my interfaith quandary--where I now feel comfortable with what I am as a religious person. And I owe that comfort to something I've learned from Unitarian Universalism. If you persist in maintaining a perspective on religion that embraces everything that is good and welcomes everyone who comes to seek it, eventually you will believe in it. Your perspective becomes your faith.

When I look at what my religious life is all about--the connection between my inner journey and my outer connection to this community--I see that my religion is no longer a question of identity. Rather it is the search for that which is *beyond* identity--for what we share that is common to all of us, for what it is about life that cannot be divided, for what is universal and true. The Unitarian Universalist way identifies itself with what makes us whole, not separate, and in that distinction religious identity politics dissolve. And that is a good thing.

Ofelia Lachtman's story, *Pepita Talks Twice*, teaches a similar lesson. Pepita, with the fervor of one who wants to be one way or another, decides she will speak only English--even though everyone else keeps telling her it's good to be bilingual. She learns early, and with a minimum of pain, that knowing two languages is good, and that she does not need to choose. And neither do we.

Thirty percent of Americans may choose a new religion for themselves. And that choice--reflecting the intensity and the need of the personal quest--is one we can respect. But faith transformations are not *only* conversions from one religious identity to another. There is another faith transformation, which we are entering here. It is marked not by the drama of conversion but by the slow-growing wisdom that results from the search for wholeness. It is concerned not with identity but with universal truth, which goes beyond borders and divisions. It is uncharted territory for many of us, whose struggle for identity has become part of who we are. But that struggle, at least for me, is precisely what I need to give up if my true self is what I hope to find.

The transformation we seek is one that brings us home to our true selves, where we grow beyond struggle and break out of narrow definitions of who we are. Instead, we grow open to that which is beyond all narrow definitions--of religion or of people. In that frontier is where we find the faith we seek.

Our faith is something new, for all of us. For whether you are visiting this church for the first time this Sunday, or have been worshipping here for thirty years, you are--as we all are--evolving constantly, arriving at new perspectives all the time. Our faith is a transforming one, not because it asks you to renounce your past, but because it asks you to be open to growth, to change, to a deepening appreciation of life and to participation in universal truths. Our faith will change you, not convert you, to a way of life that makes hope a reality because transformation is within everyone's reach. May each of us gain the wisdom our path can teach us, widening our perspective, renewing ourselves every day in the truth that we are whole, we are free, we are true to our true selves.

Resources used to prepare this sermon include Stephen J. Dubner, "Choosing My Religion," *The New York Times Magazine*, Sunday, March 31, 1996; and Ofelia Dumas Lachtman, *Pepita Talks Twice* (Houston: Piñata Books, 1995).

CELEBRATING SEASONS

KEEPING UP WITH THE DEAD

November 1, 1998

While I was picking up the candy skulls at my neighborhood Oaxacan bakery this week, I got into a conversation with a woman who works there. Normally very reserved, she became talkative when I told her I wanted the candies because we were having a Day of the Dead fiesta at our church. "In Oaxaca we use these skulls," she told me, "to give to our friends when we seek their forgiveness." This was a new twist on the meaning of the holiday, since I'd assumed that these pure sugar, virtually inedible candies were used to entice the spirits of the dead, not to rebuild friendships with the living.

It's strange. A time set aside to contemplate death becomes an exercise in relatedness. There are many of us in this room today who are contemplating death without the help of a holiday. Some grieving and learning to move on in life, others seeing the horizon of their mortality, fending off illness, hurtling into old age, all of us sensing the limit and the mystery that envelop us.

Finality is impossible to accept all at once. Grieving helps us to move forward, gaining acceptance intermittently, adapting to a new reality, finding a new way of being in the world. The death of a loved one is nothing less than a new orientation to life itself.

The philosopher Hannah Arendt once observed that when someone we love dies, we must learn to form a *new* relationship with that person. The dead are gone, but they come back because we don't forget them. We carry within us memories and feelings, and we carry *on* new conversations and intimacies with the ones we have loved. There is a sense in which they never leave, even though it is real that they have also gone forever. Our new relationship is modified and internal, but we should not underestimate its power to shape us and give direction to our lives.

Many years ago, while I was minister of a church in New England, one of the members of my congregation died very suddenly at the age of sixty-two. A swift and lethal heart attack overtook him at home; he died on the way to the hospital. By the time I got there, he was only a dead body in a room, but I sat there alone with him for a few minutes anyway, not wanting him to be disposed of too quickly.

His wife, a no-nonsense Yankee realist just like he was, saw no reason to hang around. She was someone who would grieve in private for a long time to come. I don't know why I stayed--perhaps out of the need to do something when there was nothing left to do. Whatever the reason, those moments alone with him allowed me to see that he was truly dead, and I was truly sorry he was gone.

This man was something of a cipher in life. Brilliant but disturbingly unassuming, he sold insurance for a living and spent his free time studying philosophy and religion. He looked after me and I needed looking after, I can see that now, not simply because he saw to it that I had insurance, but because he shared my interests and cared about my development.

We compared notes about theologians and philosophers. He was far better read than I, and he often wrote thoughtful responses to my sermons. He was never critical, always provocative and encouraging. I learned a lot from him. What's even more compelling is that I still do. He's been dead for fifteen years and just recently I asked myself what he would have thought of the new book about Isaiah Berlin, one of his big favorites. As I read a review of it, I thought, I should read this. He still guides from within.

I only knew this man as his minister, and I cannot say who he fully was. Yet he is one of many people who may be gone but who live on in my imagination. I remember him in ways that still direct and stimulate my life. I think he would have liked to know that.

This custom of summoning the dead to come back to us, as people do for holidays such as this one, may have little to do with supernatural powers or spirits from beyond. Rather it reminds us that a good life is one in which we affect others, and are remembered by them when we are gone. We are connected in more ways than we know how to acknowledge.

Actively relating to the dead is an acquired tendency. It helps to be old enough to have lost significant people and still miss them and need them. As I turn fifty, I realize how many people who influenced me are gone now and though it is sad to lose them, they remain part of me forever. And that is not sad at all. Somehow it becomes possible to accept the finality of death, by moving on, and taking those who have departed along with me. These new relationships remind me of who I am by remembering who they were.

I was a teenager when my grandmother died, and I felt numb and frightened by grief. For years this death was like a page torn out of a book, ragged and missing. But I loved my grandmother; and I knew her well enough that once I was ready, I formed a new relationship with her. Now I think of her with affection for the specific ways in which she touched my life: the things she made, the music she enjoyed, the recipes I still use once in a great while. Memories of her remind me of who I am, not just in genetic disposition or looks, but in the culture that shaped me, in the way I experience family and relatedness, in the likes and dislikes that define my view of the world.

For years after she was widowed, my grandmother would spend the weekend with our family. Saturday nights she would watch her favorite television show, Lawrence Welk. It was my duty to watch it with her. I was an adolescent; this felt like my hour of penance. I hated everything about the Lawrence Welk show, the polka music, the sappy humor, the all too familiar immigrant accents. My grandmother was a very sentimental woman, and the music would invariably move her to tears, while she lamented the untimely death of her husband. I had a hard time with it.

Now when I think about that time I spent with my grandmother, I see it very differently. Those Saturday nights imprinted me with precious memories that I relive myself these days. I am moved by how much she loved her husband, for theirs was a companionable marriage. She succeeded in living on her own after he died, but she always missed him. The tears on Saturday night were her tribute to him.

At thirteen I was too much of a musical snob to want to be reminded that I come from polka-loving stock, but today I see it as part of who I am. Those dreaded Saturday nights are now memories I keep, transformed by time and age into reminders of who I am and who I want to be.

In time it's no longer sad to think of those who are gone. And if holidays like this one point to a greater truth, when it's not sad anymore it's almost fun. We'd rather feel surrounded by the people we remember than feel alone. And if we learn to talk with the dead, we never really are alone. Death may be final and loss may be great, but the continuity of life nurtures connections that play by different rules, and no one is ever completely gone as long as someone remembers.

One of the privileged experiences I've had as a minister is to have known many people who have died, perhaps many more than someone else my age would have known. For any of us, to belong to a church like ours is to know and relate to people of all ages, and to expose ourselves to the cycles of life more frequently than we would outside this community. For me it means that there are many people, some I knew well, others not well at all, who make up a veritable small town of the dead, who go on in my memory. It's not the least bit depressing. They're always with me. Like the man from my church back in New England, they watch over me and influence me. They create an awareness of the continuity of life and death that I could have no other way. To remember them seems like a sacred act for that reason.

The finality of death and the loss we must bear are tasks that take everything we have to complete. Yet life seems to teach us that if we accept what death demands of us, we will learn that it is not the end of everything we value or love. There are no ways to bypass the work of grieving. But when we have done all we can do, we discover that all is not lost to us, ever.

The dead do come back to us, to guide us and remind us of who we are, and where we have come from. By remembering them and keeping up with them we join them in the continuity of life and the cycles that connect us to each other. In such good company, it's as if we could go on forever.

A SERMON FOR THANKSGIVING

November 24, 1996

Well, we made it. We survived another year and now it's time for Thanksgiving. Time makes refugees of us all. Whether it's been a good year or a hard one, the one thing we can say is that we're still here.

Maya Angelou's words may be raw but they are to the point:

Thank you, Lord.
I want to thank you, Lord
For life and all that's in it
Thank you for the day
And for the hour and for the minute
I know many are gone,
I'm still living on,
I want to thank You.

We are thankful just to be alive. The Pilgrims, who survived a harrowing ocean crossing and the punishing seasons of their new home land, were thankful just to be alive. The little girl Magda, the refugee in the story we heard earlier in the service, was thankful just to be free and safe. The rest of us, no matter what we have, are thankful just to be here another year. Thanksgiving makes refugees of us all. Or at least, it should.

Thanksgiving is the one time each year when we give thanks for life. It is the most elemental, perhaps the most spiritual, holiday of the year. Earlier this fall I had an adventure which, while it might seem tame to most of you, was sufficiently arduous for me that I got back in touch with that elemental feeling of being glad just to be alive. I took a boat trip out to Santa Cruz, one of the Channel Islands, to go snorkeling for the first time. What next, you might ask yourselves, as you brace yourself for yet another account of my outdoor water exploits.

Anyway, I haven't spent much time on the ocean. A few ferry rides over to Martha's Vineyard and Nantucket, and more recently, Catalina, just about cover the territory for me. So I didn't know what to expect when I boarded the much smaller boat headed out twenty-five miles to the west of Ventura Harbor. It was October and the seas were rough, churned up by the Santa Ana winds. Many were seasick, as the boat rocked and waves drenched the deck with icy spray.

It could have been a horrible experience, but it wasn't. Something about managing to surmount the distress of the journey-- thankfully I was not one of those who got sick, although I easily could have been--surfaced early and stayed with me throughout the day and the weeks to follow.

"I know many are gone,/ I'm still living on ...." We finally arrived at the shores of Santa Cruz Island, where the sun was shining and the hills were dry and still. And I understood that such passages are cleansing, stripping away in an amazingly short time all pretense of control and security, leaving us, shaky pilgrims in wet suits, thanking the Lord to have made it to shore.

I know I exaggerate. But I couldn't help thinking about my great-grandparents and their children, and the ordeals they underwent to make it to this shore. A couple of years ago I tried to find something out about their journey.

The genealogical library at the Mormon Temple on Santa Monica Boulevard contains passenger lists from the boats that came over in the early 1900's. I couldn't make any definitive identifications of my own family: a great grandfather, who came to this country with eleven children and no spouse, or my grandmother, who brought with her from Budapest a silver spoon and little else. They're all there somewhere, their identities buried in the lists of passengers who traveled in steerage, who left everything behind and had nothing to lose. They started over here, with nothing but their lives.

I thought about them on the return trip from Santa Cruz Island. How refugees like them have come here in waves for hundreds of years. What Thanksgiving must mean to those who are glad just to be alive.

The night I returned home from my big ocean adventure, I lay down to sleep, the motion of the boat still rocking in some part of my nervous system, and I was feeling glad just to be alive. I don't suppose we were ever in any real danger, although even experienced sailors agreed it was a rocky trip. But something about having made it home stimulated my awareness that these days are not meant to be taken for granted. Each day we lay down to sleep, safe and sound, is a day for thanksgiving.

> Thank you, Lord …
> Thank you for the day
> And for the hour and for the minute.

What is so exhilarating about experiences that make us thankful just to be alive is that they remind us what is important in life. We remember that our lives are a gift, pure and simple. There are many other gifts for which we are thankful when we stop to think about it--the experiences of love and friendship, of family and children, of work and creativity, of well-being and pleasure--and we should give thanks for them also.

But this year, for some reason, I resist taking inventory of what I like in my life. I want to see Thanksgiving differently this time around. I want to say, I give thanks unconditionally, no matter what my life is like this year, unconditionally, because I am glad just to be alive.

So this year I have friends and I feel well and I like my work and all is fine. I don't want to take any of it for granted. But neither do I want to say that life is only good when these or other *things* are part of it. What if I were a refugee, whose life depended on leaving so many things behind? Would I not still be thankful just to be alive?

And are we not all refugees, in one manner or another, as we travel from year to year in our lives? The people we must leave behind, the suffering none of us is spared, the adjustments and the accommodations we must make to the changing circumstances of life; all these conditions affect us, make survivors of us, sooner or later.

> I know many are gone,
> I'm still living on,
> I want to thank You.

You may think it is strange to talk about ourselves as survivors. Those who are survivors know that gratitude for being alive is mixed with grief and guilt and a sense of loss. Such sadness is the emotional undertow of every holiday, and it is part of what life is like for us all. But it is also why it is so important to give thanks. Giving thanks is our way of staying whole, despite the trials and losses we all endure.

To give thanks to be alive is to acknowledge the gift that each of us receives, unconditionally and innocently, and to experience this reality in whatever way it comes to us. That is where each of us starts, refugees from some cosmic process much larger than anything we get to see from here, tossed about, exhilarated, occasionally queasy, and always glad to have arrived at the shore of the present moment.

So many people, especially ones who follow a spiritual path like ours, seem to like Thanksgiving better than any other holiday of the year. There are several obvious reasons why that might be. You don't have to shop for gifts. You do not need to belong to any particular religion to celebrate it. And you don't even really have to do very much at all to experience it.

You can sit on the beach and offer your thanks to the ocean. You can sit at the table and say grace for your food. You can stay home and be quiet or travel and be part of the crowd. There really isn't any one way to do it the right way. You just need to give thanks and you've done what really matters this time.

I think that is why people like this holiday so much. They know what to do with it and it is simple and straight to the point.

> Thank you, Lord. I want to thank you, Lord
> For life and all that's in it.

That's all it is, and yet that is everything, for those whose lives have brought them this year, to this time, to this holiday; refugees from every place you can think of, every life an epic of struggle and survival; here at last, alive, safe and sound, ready to give thanks and live for whatever the future may bring.

Resources used to prepare this sermon include Maya Angelou, "Thank you, Lord" in *And Still I Rise* (New York: Random House, 1978).

A SEASON TURNS

December 23, 2001

No one has to convince me that human beings can grow out of touch with our connection to nature. My own life offers abundant examples of just how that happens. A few days before Christmas, my husband David and I went out to buy our Christmas tree here in California. After visiting two huge tree lots and cruising the streets of Venice in search of another, we still had not found what we wanted.

There were no small trees left, and small was what we had to have. I would have compromised just to get it over with, but David, ever the architect, declared that he had not seen a single tree that "excited" him, so we went home empty-handed. Connecting to nature had nothing to do with getting a tree, for either of us.

I don't know when the noble fir, the oldest and most enduring symbol of the winter holidays, stopped being simply a tree and started being a design statement. But I do know that we are not alone in having a certain image of what our tree is supposed to look like. People impose all sorts of expectations on Mother Nature's performance. This is only one of many ways in which we veer away from the meaning of the season. Too much becomes over-determined, and we become over-wrought. We think only of what we are supposed to do to make the season happen. But the truth is that the season always turns whether we do anything or not.

That is not enough for us, however. G.K. Chesterton observed, "We tend to tire of the most eternal splendours, and a mark on our calendar, or a crash of bells at midnight maybe, reminds us that we have only recently been created." We need to invent observances and add our human touch before we can appreciate the great natural drama that unfolds continuously all around us.

These are necessary activities and touches. Actually, they may help us relate to nature in ways we never could before. I did not go camping, after all, until polar fleece and Gore-Tex were invented. So even though we may add layers of embellishment, we never get completely out of touch.

Our observance of these holidays, the winter solstice and Christmas, offers ancient and deeply rooted expressions of the human experience of the cycles of nature--not just what is happening outside, but inside ourselves as well. The season turns and carries us along with it.

Some images of the season are nearly universal. Their meaning is simple: life continues, even during the harshest time of the year. And new life is on its way. The human affinity for evergreen during this bleak season is nearly universal too. According to a Cherokee tale, the Great Sun granted the "gift of green forever" to the pine, the fir, the spruce, the holly, and the laurel for their faithful waiting on the Great Sun's return. In ancient Rome, people brought evergreens into their homes as decorations for New Year's celebrations. The Christmas tree itself, which first appeared in Germany in the seventeenth century, undoubtedly evolved from these origins. The Christian church, however, initially rejected these celebrations of nature as backward and heathenish. But the efforts of the church to eradicate pagan customs failed spectacularly. Finally it modified them to reflect Christian theology, a much more effective strategy, and appropriated the popular Christmas tree as a Christian symbol.

Christian legend links the Christmas tree not only to Jesus himself, who is named tree of life and light of the world, but also to the tree of knowledge from which Adam and Eve plucked an apple, and even to the tree from which the cross was built. And there is more: according to Christian lore, on the night that Jesus was born, the rivers ran with wine and the trees stood in full blossom. The custom of decorating the tree with flowers and fruit, or ornaments to look like them, neatly incorporates every reference--pagan and Christian-- imaginable.

All of this teaches a really good lesson: that whatever twists we humans put on the persistent, pervasive symbols of the season, they still lead us back to nature. So put your silver artificial tree in the window, as my neighbors did, or decorate it with ceramic dogs, as we do, or with sky blue swags and Styrofoam snowflakes, as I saw at the Water Garden. Stray as far from what nature intended as your heart desires. You'll still end up with the return of the Great Sun, the continuity of life and the hope of the New Year.

It happens whether you do anything or not. It happens with or without your help. It happens even if you sleep through it. It happens because nature carries us through life and brings us renewal, whether we decorated our home or not.

That may sound rather optimistic for a year of outrageous natural tragedy and one in which a war of questionable purpose continues to drag on and on. We could not be more conscious that there is much that is not renewable--so many human lives, a sense of safety and innocence about our world--and our hearts reverberate with the distress all around us. Simple holiday tasks become difficult when life has become difficult.

A poem by Delmore Schwartz speaks to this condition. He writes of dusk approaching when a calm voice tells him,

> Wait: wait: wait as if you had always waited
> And as if it had always been dark.

Somewhere in that waiting, he realizes, is "hope, / and the pain of hope, / and the patience of hope."

During difficult times, we wait. We wait whether we want to or not. We wait because it is all we can do. We wait because when there is nothing we can do, time will change us anyway. While we wait, we hope. Hope is enough.

Whatever these holidays mean to you, and however you choose to enter into them, their timeless meanings prevail. Life continues, and new life will come in all its many forms. The days grow longer, and the earth will renew itself. Love appears, and people are reborn. The New Year arrives, and the passage of time revives us.

In the Cherokee solstice story, the plants and trees wither from frost, their leaves drop, and though they struggle to stay awake to greet the return of the Great Sun, they don't make it. Only a few hardy ones can last through the cold night. But the Great Sun returns anyway, giving the gift of warm light to the hardy plants and to the sleeping ones too. It is the same for us.

The lesson of these winter holidays is that time and nature will make us whole, and we don't have to do everything ourselves. Our job is to wait and to hope and to let the cycles of life and creation do the rest. To celebrate the season is to remember the simple truth that we belong to nature, a truth that is both obvious and somehow hard for us to grasp. But when we forget, we have these customs to help us experience it.

I defaulted on the Christmas tree selection. David went and got one, though I forgot to ask him if he was excited by it. I'm content to have a small green tree in our living room, which can use a little extra color this time of year.

The work we make of the holidays is rooted in the joy of life, its resilience and its wholeness. Somehow, even when we don't realize it, the joy is there, and that touch of green, even the unexciting but necessary tree, helps us to feel it.

This version of *A Season Turns* appeared in *Quest*, a publication of the Unitarian Universalist Association Church of the Larger Fellowship, December 2005. Delmore Schwartz, "During December's Death" is in *Selected Poems: Summer Knowledge* (New York: New Directions, 1967).

THE NAME OF THE SOUL

December 8, 1996

The Jewish rabbis who assembled the holy books which became the Hebrew Bible were also the arbiters of Jewish tradition, and they did not have much to say about Hanukkah. The evolution of this festival remains mysterious. The Talmud barely addresses its practice and few actually celebrated it until the late nineteenth century.

Jewish scholar Arthur Waskow speculates that the rabbis did not approve of the Maccabean approach to Jewish life. For even though the Maccabees led a successful revolt against their Syrian oppressors, they were well assimilated into Greek culture. As models of Jewish identity, there was a lot missing. So traditional Jews did not value or promote their story.

Instead, Greeks and Jews who had adopted Greek ways recorded the story of Hanukkah in Greek scripture--part of the Christian Bible known as the Apocrypha. It is instructive for us to understand that a holiday that now emphasizes Jewish identity and solidarity was originally dismissed by the rabbis and preserved by the Greeks. What made Hanukkah a distinctively Jewish holiday, affirming Jewish history and resistance to assimilation, was its dependence on non-Jewish culture.

In an added twist to the meaning of the celebration, Hanukkah resurfaced into contemporary Judaism only when barriers between Christians and Jews dissolved sufficiently to allow them to read each other's holy books. So Jews, reading Christian texts for the first time in the nineteenth century, rediscovered the story of Hanukkah. They reappropriated it into their tradition and creatively interpreted it as a spiritual and cultural event, augmenting their array of holidays.

It is ironic that a story validating Jewish identity could only have survived outside Jewish tradition. But there is an important lesson in that irony. It makes us wonder what religious identity is, and how it persists. Perhaps religious identity, which so many of us take to be immutable, and even genetic, is actually an artificial construct.

Perhaps it only exists by mutual agreement to preserve differences and to maintain boundaries. Perhaps it is a blessing and a curse.

Religious identity is a powerful force. It distinguishes us. It divides us. It concerns us here, because most of us have questioned our identity and have chosen to push ourselves beyond it, even though we are not always certain how that is done. Many of us are searching for a meaningful expression of transcendent values, but don't know how they relate to what we've always thought about religion.

Religious identity has told us who we are, it gave us a name, which is convenient and sometimes even comforting, but it has also held us back. If you are one of the many people who joins this congregation on Sundays and wonders what you are doing here, you are probably trying to push beyond the definitions and boundaries imposed by your religious identity. You are probably searching for something beyond or beneath the definitions and the divisions. It's uncharted territory and not always a comfortable experience.

But you are almost certainly in the right place. I often reflect on religious identity during the holiday season, because questions come up for me every year, as they do for many of you. What does it mean to be who we are now, given that we may have started out as Jewish or Christian or Muslim or Hindu? Or what does it mean to be here, in church, if we started out in families that avoided religious affiliations and gave us nothing to accept or reject?

For me, the religious identity question is always reduced to, what does it mean to be half Jewish and half Christian? Do they cancel each other out? Sometimes. Do they enrich my religious life? Yes, if you agree with my family that the only way I could reconcile these two aspects of my religious identity was to become a professional.

I have spent most of my life asking myself how I can have two religious identities. And they are weak identities, I should add. On the Jewish side, no one ever spoke Yiddish, went to temple, or celebrated any holidays. On the Christian side, they married Jews. I was brought up in a Unitarian home by parents who cheerfully embraced religious humanism, and who were puzzled by my dilemma. So I have had to work things out on my own. Or through my work, some might say.

When I study the origins of Jewish or Christian traditions, I feel like a field worker among an alien, though interesting people. Perhaps I have too much distance on it, but I have never felt that either way could be my way. As a lifelong Unitarian Universalist, I've never felt required to define myself in Christian or Jewish terms, but as a lifelong Jewish Christian hybrid, I've longed for greater identification with these roots. But it's just not there. I always end up in the uncharted territory, along with you, because there is simply no going back.

If that is our predicament, then the Hanukkah story may hold a somewhat different lesson for us than it does for Jews. For Jews, it is a reminder of who they are and how strong their faith can be. The Jewish faith is a dynamic, unfolding drama of the relationship between a particular people and their God, their oppressors, and their vision of a promised land. The story of Hanukkah winds its way through years of exile, buried in Greek scripture, only to resurface in an environment where dialogue and discovery were possible.

The Hanukkah story itself speaks to the timelessness and resilience of a coherent faith tradition. It also speaks to those of us who do not belong to that tradition, because it shows us that outsiders can play a meaningful part in it as well. Our part is to protect the pluralistic environment in which religions flourish and develop free from oppression, to be good neighbors in a world where tolerance offers shelter to everyone. Anyone who wants to practice tolerance should know and understand the history of the Jewish people.

I chose the two stories I read this morning because they illustrate the power that outsiders can have by being good neighbors to people of other faiths. In the story I read to the children, the Christian merchant places a higher value on his fidelity to his Jewish friend than to improving his own circumstances, even when they become dire. After the crisis has passed, the Christian and the Jew share their wealth, not just the jewels that the Christian had safeguarded, but the loyalty and trust that they gave to each other. In this Jewish folktale, we find a positive example of people who go beyond their religious identity and practice transcendent values together.

Similarly, the story of the two Jewish sisters who find refuge in an Italian town provides an inspiring example of bonds that transcend religious identity. It is the Christian neighbors who protect these two women. And it is the two Jewish women who choose their love for their new home over the opportunity to live in the promised land.

Each of these stories suggests the possibilities inherent in the bold and often courageous act of going beyond the conventions prescribed by religious identity. Each of these stories suggests to us that there may be more religious value in being good neighbors than in being good Jews or good Christians or good Unitarian Universalists. What we may be seeking is a religious value we identify with actions that express qualities that go beyond those of loyalty to one group over another.

Perhaps what we are trying to find is something that is real and without boundaries, true and without self-interest, sustaining and not just for ourselves. We suspect that you cannot put a name on a soul, and that religious identity alone may not give us faith. We are searching for a religion that is beyond religions, beyond identity, creed or history.

And that is why we often wonder what we are doing. We've never done it before. But we've known it all along. So have all people of every religion, when they have acted on the deepest convictions and intuitions they sense in themselves.

The Hasidic meditation we heard earlier tells us this is so. All souls are one, because each is a spark of the original soul. When you go deep enough, you pass through definitions, and divisions and conflicts burn off like morning fog in good strong sun.

Truth is often simple. What does it take to enter into the presence of the Eternal? According to the Jewish prophet Micah, only to be just and kind and to live in quiet fellowship with your God. If we could all just do that, our religion would have taught us well.

Reading the story of Hanukkah this year, I realized that instead of feeling that familiar envy for a religious community that knows who it is and where it wants to go, I arrived at a deeper appreciation of what we are trying to do here. For when you make a commitment, as we have, to understand and respect diversity of religious expression, what you gain may be more than what you lose.

It is true that you leave the security of a consistent religious identity and all the certainty of belonging that it bestows. But it is also true that you become a good neighbor, giving shelter and practicing tolerance. You become one with those people of all faiths who know that whatever your identity or lack of one, there is no name for the soul, because all souls are one; there is only the reach beyond the names and the definitions that divide us and keep us apart from each other.

We often say here that we respect the wisdom of all religious traditions. But if we don't explain what we mean, such declarations sound glib at best, even hypocritical. We don't jump around from religion to religion, mixing up beliefs, many of them contradicting each other, pouring them into some synthesis. We don't steal another people's faith, out of context, without regard for their history and their tradition.

What we do instead is this: we look for the wisdom that lies *beyond* religion, and is expressed in one way or another by *every* religion. We listen for the truth that all souls are one. We work to be good neighbors, to do our part to assure shelter and tolerance to everyone, whatever their religion might be.

And we live our lives, perhaps a little more exposed and vulnerable, without the security and the protection of religious identity, but safe, ultimately, in the knowledge that there is no name for the soul. For where we want to go, all souls are one.

Resources used to prepare this sermon include Arthur Waskow, *Seasons of Our Joy: A Celebration of Modern Jewish Renewal* (Boston: Beacon Press, 1982); and "The Good Neighbor," a traditional Jewish folktale adapted by Josepha Sherman in *Rachel the Clever* (Atlanta: August House, 1993).

TRUTH FROM THE ROAD

Palm Sunday, April 5, 1998

The journey Jesus took to Jerusalem in the last week before his death did nothing to cool down the controversy that accompanied him wherever he went. It started in Jericho, where two blind men appealed to him for a healing touch, which he gave, despite the heated protests of the large crowd following him. Once in Jerusalem, where he arrived in humble fashion on the back of a donkey, he went straight to the Temple and threw out the money changers. He told parables about tax collectors and prostitutes entering the kingdom of God, much to everyone's shock and dismay. His last sermons spoke of loving your neighbor, while nailing the scribes and the Pharisees as outrageous hypocrites. He depicted the Last Judgment as a reckoning on the generosity and childlike faith of those who welcomed the stranger, fed the hungry, clothed the naked, and comforted the sick.

"I tell you solemnly," preached Jesus, "in so far as you neglected to do this to one of the least of these, you neglected to do it to me."

This is one of the most difficult and controversial passages of the gospel narratives. It angers and challenges people today just as it did during Jesus' time. His teachings set impossible standards and appear to lack prudence and credibility. Yet his teachings lift the human moral imagination out of the rut of convention into a higher realm of compassion and truth. We have only to look to variations on the social gospel, from the base communities of Central America to liberation movements embraced by oppressed people in our own country, to appreciate the power and the inspiration of their source. It was Jesus, on the road to Jerusalem, only a few days before his death.

A couple of weeks ago the director of Daybreak, a drop-in center for mentally ill homeless women, called me to see if I would perform a memorial service for one of their clients, Nilda. She had been murdered here in Santa Monica. Although her body had not yet been found, someone had already confessed to the crime.

We were told that Nilda's body had been thrown into a dumpster, and the police were searching the landfills. It was a tragic end to a difficult life, what I knew of it. She had just managed to find housing, after months of living on the street, only to be killed by her roommate.

Normally when I prepare a memorial service, I interview the people who knew and loved the one who has died, so that the intimate life story becomes part of the tribute. I had trouble finding out much about Nilda. I wasn't even sure how to spell her last name. I didn't know anything about her family, if she had one. Someone thought she might have had children. The staff people who knew her maintained strict confidentiality about her troubles. I heard vague and wistful comments about how sad it was that she had finally found a home, how she had befriended so many other homeless women in her time outside, and how hopeful she was about the future. With only scraps of information, I put together a service. It was to be held outdoors in the Rose Garden in Palisades Park.

That morning I drove to the place where I thought the service was to be held, but saw no one. Thinking I must be mistaken, I drove up and down Ocean Avenue looking for the people I knew I would recognize. I saw no Rose Garden and I saw no people. It was time for the service to begin and I was still driving around in my car, looking for it.

I have never ever been late for a religious service that I was to lead, and knowing this was happening made me frantic. I was afraid that someone might interpret my being late as a casual attitude towards this somber but loosely organized outdoor gathering. I questioned it myself. What good were all the services I had conducted for all the people eulogized in the comfort of our sanctuary if I "neglected to do [the same] for one of the least of these," to use the words of Jesus in judgment on myself.

When I finally located a park groundskeeper, she sent me off to a barren thicket not far from where I had originally stopped. Ready to apologize for my apparent lack of respect for the deceased, I arrived at the service embarrassed and breathless. Almost no one else was there yet--her fellow mourners were still walking to the site from the scattered shelters, agencies, and alleys that make up their world, perpetually late and out of time.

But three people were there, waiting for something to happen. They were Nilda's daughter, mother, and former husband. Nilda's mother had flown in from the Midwest. Shaky and confused, she admitted she still had hope that her daughter would be found alive. Nilda's daughter lived with her father. They told me there was another daughter too, an infant who lived with the family in the Midwest.

I began to get a glimpse of Nilda's world. Drug-addicted and mentally ill, she was unable to maintain herself in family life. Until she died, none of them knew where she was. Now they gathered in a circle formed by homeless men and women, joined by staff people from Step Up on Second and Ocean Park Community Center, to say a final goodbye.

What happened next was moving and instructive. Nilda may have been a lost soul to some of us, a woman whose story was sealed in confidential files and long empty episodes of oblivion, but she was an anchor for many others. One after another, out of the circle we had formed around a bucket of cut flowers, people came forward to talk about how she had touched their lives. They told their stories, they wept in grief, and they prayed for her spirit. And I realized that the depth of this life was not for me to know, but it was there all the same, for the least of these as well as for the greatest.

And I thought about all the lost souls, some dazed, others cunning, most just trying to survive, and how their lives were not that different from any other's. Take one missing person with an obscure past, ask those who care to come forward, and see what happens. Some are loved; others are alone. Some have good intentions and try hard, as Nilda's friends repeatedly affirmed, while others give up and are lost.

The truth of their lives is the same as the truth of our lives. There was a lot more to Nilda than I could ever have known. There is more to us than anyone realizes.

The truth that Jesus preached is that it does not matter who you are, or even whether you have lived a life that others admire or envy. The truth is that all this outward appearance and posturing mean nothing. The scribes and the Pharisees are no better than the tax collectors and the prostitutes. The pious can be hypocrites and the weak can be stronger in faith than anyone. To love God, Jesus would say, is to be humbled by these examples and to love your neighbor as yourself. Perhaps what he meant is that we should respect the depth and fullness of life in all people, whoever they may be.

To affirm the worth and dignity of all persons, as our Unitarian Universalist principles guide us, is to recognize that goodness comes in many forms, some of them unlikely. That is why Jesus repeatedly dropped whatever he was doing to minister to the afflicted, the lost, and the discarded people along his way. That is the message his life still speaks to many of us. What we have to give to the least of these is the true measure of our own souls.

Our community can make good use of our desire to help, to heal, and to extend ourselves to those who are nearly beyond our reach. What is not wise or even safe for us to do on our own we can do together, through community services and group activities. I can see that through my involvement with Ocean Park Community Center, I have opportunities to minister to people whom I would have met no other way. I am always touched by these experiences. They make me a better minister.

In the coming week, the Christian world prepares for the highest holy day of the year. Beginning with the momentous arrival of Jesus in Jerusalem, the days hasten a tragic drama of judgment and betrayal. Jesus paid dearly for his teachings.

Yet Christians have brought meaning to his life and death, by seeing his message as God's gift to humanity, a way to look at each other and a way to live our lives striving to be better people. Our own liberal religious tradition has chosen to understand his life not all that differently. Setting aside doctrinal questions about his divinity and the belief in eternal life, we are left with the example of one bold, mysterious, and prophetic teacher who saw the worth and dignity in every person, no matter who they were.

Nilda's life, short and doomed though it may have been, achieves a greater worth and dignity by looking at it as Jesus might have seen her. For her goodness may mean more, ultimately, to this world, than what so many others, comfortable, sane, and healthy, may be able to do no matter how much time they are given. This was a woman who reached out through layers of pain, addiction, poverty, and despair, to make friends with her neighbors, the homeless and the lost, and to bring them hope.

I know. I was at her service. That is how she is remembered. And she will never be forgotten.

FREE FOR LIFE

Passover and Easter Sunday, April 12, 1998

Today we celebrate Easter and Passover together as if these two sacred Christian and Jewish observances were actually part of the same tradition--a tradition that includes even older observances of seasonal rebirth belonging to the pagan religions--and to do that requires a certain distance from them all.

That distance is both dangerous and instructive. To commingle separate religious events without recognizing their differences could suggest that we don't know what the differences are, or worse, don't care, and that would be intolerant and cavalier. More often, however, we put our energy into articulating differences so well, that we forget that recognizing universal similarities can also show respect and understanding. And finding universal similarities can bring us closer to the meaning of the season and the core message of all celebrations.

In that spirit, the merging of the spring holidays into one weekend poses an opportunity to step back and look at them together, and to celebrate a message common to each. It is a message so fundamental that religious people have invariably turned to miracles, metaphors, and epic narratives to express it, as if the simple truth were not enough.

They say that Jesus died, but he didn't really die; even after he died, he still lived. They say that the Hebrew people triumphed in the long journey from slavery to freedom because they kept going even when they were tired and hungry and doubted they'd ever reach the promised land. They say that new life, whether it is in the growth of your garden or in the birth of your children only comes because what is old and tired lets itself die to make room for the new. And they say that rebirth can come even to those who are old and tired and ready to give up hope that there is anything left in life for them.

It's not that they all say the same thing: they don't. But in one way or another, the message is one of hope, of endurance, and of believing, sometimes despite all the evidence, that life triumphs over despair.

It's about believing that life triumphs over despair. It's not about the differences that distinguish Christian faith and Jewish identity and pagan ritual, lively and relevant though they may be today. It's about being alive--and being willing to trust that is reason enough in itself to celebrate.

There's a Buddhist story that teaches an original lesson about the human tendency to dwell so much on our differences that we lose our grasp of the truth: "Some years ago, a leading Tibetan Buddhist teacher met with a Korean Zen master for dharma combat--an encounter that tests and challenges each master's understanding of Buddhist teaching. As the Tibetan lama sat fingering his prayer beads and murmuring a mantra, the younger Korean Zen master began the exchange by reaching inside his robe, drawing out an orange and holding it up. In a defiant and challenging tone, he asked, 'What is this?'"

"It was the classic Zen question and the Korean master waited to pounce on any response that would betray ignorance. The Tibetan simply sat quietly without saying anything in reply. The Korean moved closer, held the orange under the lama's nose and repeated his question: 'What is this?'"

"The Tibetan lama bent over to discuss the situation with his translator. The two Tibetans talked for several minutes, then the translator spoke to everyone in the room: 'The lama says, "What is the matter with him? Don't they have oranges where he comes from?" The dharma combat went no further.'"

I tell this story to suggest that what we are here to celebrate today is as obvious and as resistant to debate as the orange the Zen master showed to the Tibetan.

We celebrate life. We celebrate renewal. We celebrate our faith in the cycles that carry us through every disappointment, every loss, every failure, and every disbelief that threatens to undermine our freedom to love life exactly as it is right now. This spring holiday season reminds us that wherever we come from, we can believe the simple affirmation that life is good.

It's not always obvious or easy that this is true. A member of our congregation recently told me that her greatest challenge as a parent is to convince her teenage daughter that life is not meaningless.

She wants her daughter to know that there is a reason to hope, not to despair, and that this is the foundation of her faith. What she--and all of us--are seeking is a way to have faith--not a faith in one religion or another, but a faith in life. In what evidence will we place our trust that even with all its sorrow, injustice, and randomness, this life still has meaning? It's a tough question to answer.

I don't have faith in everything. I don't have faith that everything works out for the best, or ultimately acquires meaning, or cannot simply be senseless or cruel. Some aspects of our world are meaningless, and no amount of faith can turn them into something I can accept, even if others do. It's a harsh reality. And yet, we see all around us evidence that people experience life as meaningful and good when they trust life and allow themselves to grow.

People undergo large and small transformations: changing a failure into a turning point, sharing a mutual loss and making a friend, accepting limitations and finding depth, surviving suffering and glimpsing transcendence. Not always. But the fact that it happens, and happens regularly, sometimes even cyclically, is the basis of our faith in life. All is never lost.

The tragedies of our time have given us chilling evidence of how easily brutality rises and how much can be lost. Humanity itself is jeopardized by our own nature. But not completely. Kindness, sacrifice, and courage have also arisen, allowing humanity to go on believing in itself, and in the transforming reality of simple and trusting gestures toward one another.

There is evidence in all kinds of unlikely places. The first Sunday service I ever conducted was not in a Unitarian Universalist church. It was in the chapel of a state hospital. I was working as a student chaplain in the medical center across the street. It was my turn to fill in on Sunday for the vacationing Baptist pastor who regularly led services at the state hospital, so I had to do it.

I'd never even written a sermon before. I was told to use a biblical text, so I decided to preach on Jesus' saying, "The kingdom of God is within you." I figured that in a state institution, it was either inside people or not at all. But I didn't really know what I was doing.

The chapel was hot. There were only a few patients there for the service. When the organist played a hymn, nobody sang. Some cried, others rocked back and forth, most stayed seated, holding their heads in their hands.

I was wearing the Baptist minister's robe, a black one several sizes too big for me, and I looked ridiculous and uncomfortable. I have no idea what I said or how I managed to fill in the time. Other than these few impressions, I only remember one other part of the service. But it was memorable.

At the end of the service, at the close of the hymn, I prepared to give the closing words, a blessing. Delivering the closing words at the end of a service is a very moving experience for me. It still is. I'd never done it before then. I had watched the Baptist minister do it, however. He raised his hands, both of them, slowly, and held them high as he spoke. So I did the same.

I raised my hands, oversized sleeves of the robe hanging down in that hot old chapel, and said my blessing to the congregation. And as I stood there, I saw, much to my great surprise, my little congregation stand, raise their hands, and bless me! And I cannot tell you exactly why but I just knew right then and there that life was not meaningless. Not their lives, even if they spent them within the walls of a run-down old state hospital, and not my life either. Not because of who we were. But because of what had happened between us.

It was as if that blessing was our way of saying to each other, life is not meaningless as long as you can bless another human being. It's our way of saying to each other, the journey may be long and we may lose our way, but if we keep our faith in living, we will find our way home.

This season, we need only to remember the simple truth that all our celebrations express. Life is good. It is not easy, nor is it without suffering, pain, or death. But if we trust life, and let the goodness in it bring out the goodness in us, we will find what gives us the strength and the confidence to live fully, come all seasons, forever.

Resources used to prepare this sermon include Leo D. Defebure, "Two Hundred Years in Tibet: Glimpses in Fact and Film," *Christian Century*, March 11, 1998.

TAKING FUN SERIOUSLY

TELL YOU A STORY

October 3, 2004

What if--your imaginary friend were real? And people as different as Moonies and Unitarians knew the same hymns and sang them together while they traveled in a foreign land? What if--we could all go to the peaceable kingdom where the lion lies down with the lamb? And we told each other these stories because we realized that we needed them to stay alive?

Stories cover the gap between fantasy and reality. They awaken our imaginations to new possibilities. They give us hope when our vision fails us. They ask us "what if?" when we are stuck in what is. From the parables of Jesus to the creation myths of every culture, stories help people fashion spiritual traditions. Stories transmit intuitive truths, in colorful and even fantastic form. They build a narrative bridge between the known and the unknown. They hover between what is and "what if," making use of paradox and ambiguity to show us something we cannot know any other way.

Stories remind us of who we really are, and what the world can really be. They embody ideals. They capture mystery. They show us the surreal quality of everyday life. And they provide a subversive challenge to our assumptions about what is real.

In the story I read earlier in the service, Ruthie's parents keep telling her that Jessica, her imaginary friend, is *not* real. Their pronouncements are printed in great big bold letters on the page, conveying the full weight of parental authority. But the story proves the parents wrong, as Ruthie meets her first real friend, whose name is Jessica, their first day of school. The child navigates the path from imaginary to real without missing a step. And so the story demonstrates how the mystery and wisdom of childhood are tamper-proof. I love children's stories because they are a simple but powerful means of communication. We remember them and what they teach us. Long after you--and I--have forgotten what I said in a sermon, we remember the really good story that went with it.

I also love children's stories because I enjoy how children react to them. Children have a wonderful sense of the absurd, and so do many good children's stories. Perhaps you remember *A Tale of Three Ralphs*. It's about parents who name all their children Ralph in an effort to overcome difference and treat all their children exactly alike. Naturally this strategy leads them straight into trouble. Of all the stories I've read over many years, children seem to like that one best, despite--or perhaps because of--its sophisticated message.

Children love humor. They also seem to have an appetite for grim, dark fables, more than I do, and stories in which justice is meted out without mercy. And they show no mercy for sappy outcomes or plot contrivances that underestimate their intelligence. I've seen that too.

I was on one of my regular runs to the children's book store recently, when I realized how important these stories have become for me. I enjoy the time with the children and that's one good reason why I value the stories as I do. But I also like the stories just for themselves. They reach me on a level I do not readily access other ways. And perhaps because they do, they help me write my sermon and construct our worship service. They have become, as Catherine Farmer, our Director of Religious Education, suggested to me recently, our "story for all ages." Which is what we now call it.

Stories show us how many ways we can speak the truth. They use unpretentious language and colorful images, making them accessible to children *and* adults. They don't require scholarly footnotes or scientific research to document their claims. And because they are stories, they don't need to tell us everything. They are not comprehensive explanations, just stories.

The children's literature we use in our Sunday service can be either secular or religious, and any source is fair game. I have noticed, over the years, how these stories, whatever their origin, are the only mythical element our religious sensibility can tolerate. There is a reason for this.

Our tradition, especially the Unitarian branch of it, first articulated itself in the early nineteenth century with its emphasis on the role of reason in religious understanding. Reason overcame ignorance and superstition; reason gave rise to scientific discovery and social progress. Reason was the test of truth, and the source of wisdom. William Ellery Channing, a prominent Unitarian preacher of the time, gave voice to this point of view and applied it to reading the Bible. He declared, "Need I descend to particulars to prove that the Scriptures demand the exercise of Reason? Recollect the declarations of Christ, that he came not to send peace but a sword; that unless we eat his flesh and drink his blood we have no life in us; that we must hate father and mother, and pluck out the right eye; and a vast number of passages equally bold and unlimited." He made an important point, which he enlarged by adding that Unitarians "feel it our bounden duty to exercise our reason upon [the Bible] perpetually."

Never mind that these are stories, that Jesus spoke in parables, and that many reasonable Christians and Jews have successfully used scripture the way we use *A Tale of Three Ralphs*. Our "bounden duty" has haunted us ever since, as generations of Unitarian Universalists have exercised our reason perpetually, critically, and all too often, humorlessly, without the help of stories. We have assumed that intellectual stimulation comes from following a closely reasoned argument or a long string of ideas or statistics, but not from the imaginative leap between reality and fantasy.

If ours is a religion of reason, we might have argued, then fantasy has no place in it anyway. But the problem is not with fantasy. The problem is how to use stories and to understand in what sense they are true. Channing had good reason to be concerned about the uncritical reading of scripture, just as we do today. We all know the kind of damage people do when they interpret stories from the Bible or other sacred texts as if they were true in a literal sense. This is the problem and danger of fundamentalism.

But today we also know that stories of all kinds play an important role in transmitting values, teaching lessons, and showing us how to live. We appreciate stories because of what they can give us. As Barry Lopez writes, "The stories people tell have a way of taking care of them." Our relationship to our stories does not end with our consumption of them. We ought to care for them, as Barry Lopez writes, "and learn to give them away where they are needed." We might add, and find out what they mean to us. Understand that they have power we need.

Barry Lopez went so far as to say, "Sometimes a person needs a story more than food to stay alive." The story I read earlier--a true story, from Meg Barnhouse--is the kind of story we need if we want to stay alive today. She writes about traveling to the Taj Mahal on a bus filled with interfaith pilgrims. This unlikely group of Muslims, Hindus, Jews, Christians, Buddhists, and Moonies spent the long bus ride comparing their beliefs, telling about their loved ones, and singing.

What an amazing image she makes, of the Southern Baptists singing their "blood hymns," as she calls them, on the bus. "We had a fine time," she writes, "and we got applause from the Sikhs who were sitting behind us with their long beards, white turbans, and curved daggers on their belts." The Sikhs reciprocated with their songs, and soon the bus echoed with songs and chants from every faith tradition it contained.

"These days," she concludes, "when I hear about the peaceable kingdom where the lion will lie down with the lamb, when I read about the clamor of nations struggling toward peace, I think about the day …when Christ and Shiva clapped for each other and sang in harmony on a dusty road in a turquoise bus hung with marigolds." It's a story about saving the world, nothing less. And we need nothing more than we need that.

What if--the Southern Baptists and the Muslims could get on that bus right now? What if--we can call into being that imaginary place where people are at peace with their differences? What if--we listened to the stories that tell us this can happen because it did happen, once, to one Meg Barnhouse as she rode a turquoise bus on a dusty road from New Delhi to the Taj Mahal? And as we listened, we just knew that the story told us a truth we had known all along, and though it isn't exactly what *is* right now, it will be, if we believe in it, and take good care of it, and remember that sometimes what we imagine does indeed become real.

Resources used to prepare this sermon include Meg Barnhouse, "Rock of Ages at the Taj Mahal" in *All the Gifts of Life: Collected Meditations*, ed. Patricia Frevert (Boston: Skinner House Books, 2002); William Ellery Channing, "Unitarian Christianity" in *The Works of William Ellery Channing, D.D.* (Boston: J. Munroe & Co., 1841); and Barry Lopez, *Crow and Weasel* (New York: Farrar, Straus and Giroux, 1998).

FALLING IN

September 29, 1996

Vacation plans seem so innocent and alluring in the abstract, few of us ever anticipate that what started off as mere recreation will land us in the heart of darkness. But the adventures we choose often have hidden meanings. What may have started as a simple fantasy can quickly lead us to something we really do need to do, make clear something that was obscure; uncover the primal truth of the path we follow.

So it was for me with rowing. Having spent many years watching, from some warm dry spot, the rugged crews making their way down the chilly Charles River back in Boston, I decided to take up the sport myself, now that I'm in warm dry Los Angeles. I actually thought I might be good at it, which shows how little I knew about what I was getting into. So I spent the summer rising early in the morning, getting myself down to the marina in time for my 6:30 a.m. class.

I'm not going to tell you much about rowing today, except for this: it is a very demanding sport, requiring not just strength, which I have, but balance and coordination, which I don't. You sit atop a very light, very narrow one-person boat with only your oars for outriggers, a boat so delicate it is called a shell, and you propel yourself *backwards* through the water, using a nearly impossible-to-perfect stroke involving your legs, your back, and your arms.

It takes about eight weeks of lessons--eight weeks and about eight hours of private coaching, if you are me--to qualify to go out on your own. I made it! I did complete my "intermediate sculling" class, and after one last remedial session this week, I'm just like everyone else. I have a tremendous sense of accomplishment about having made it this far, for I had such a long way to go. From the early days, when my mind simply refused to make sense of, let alone remember, the parts of the boat for our written test, to the small ways in which I managed to *lose* some part of my boat each time I went out in it, rowing has been both a fun challenge and a psychological ordeal.

The low point, of course, was the day I fell in. Everybody falls in eventually, but I had to be the first. "Lean a little more to the left, Judith," my teacher instructed me from the authoritative distance of her powerboat, and in an effort to do exactly what she said, I tipped right over, into the warm July water. The water in the marina alone is something to fear. I found myself surfacing alongside the plastic bags, syringes, and dead life forms, trying not to swallow any. I did succeed in righting my boat quickly and got back in. My teacher did not even give me the option of returning to the dock, so I finished the class wet, wondering what had just happened to me.

I fell in. I couldn't stop telling people about it. Everyone who asked me routinely, "How are you?" that day heard me answer, "I fell in. I'm fine." Then I would launch into an extended narrative of my arduous rowing adventures, my exhilaration and anxiety transforming me into a social bore.

Falling in changed everything for me. The next few times I went out, it took all my determination to keep rowing, while an anxious voice inside my head told me not to move, leaving me paralyzed and cowering in the safety position, out in the middle of the marina. The only way to break through fear like that is to accept that you will fall in again, possibly even over and over again, because without falling in, you may never learn how to row. You may never learn anything you need to know if you are so afraid of the unknown you cannot move in any direction at all.

That is why I like the language Jim Finley uses in writing about religious faith. "Even now we hover over the bottomless abyss," he writes. "Even now we lose our footing and fall into a new, unending center." It is what we learn from falling that teaches us what really holds us up. In Finley's language, it is "a new, unending center in which we are upheld by God and not by the narrow base of our ego's self-assertion." I understand what he means, if not in the Christian sense, then at least in the rowing sense: all that struggle and effort can lead you somewhere only when you let yourself go, even if you fall in. When I understood, in the fullness of *my* being, that rowing was going to be very difficult for me, I shed *my* ego's self-assertion of my strengths and my competitive will, and humbly tumbled into the abyss. Learning to row, or seeking a faith, can only come to you if you are willing to let yourself fall in. What you find at the bottom is not what you had feared. Instead, you find some "new, unending center," as Finley writes, some confidence in yourself and in life that takes you beyond the ways you have taught yourself to cope in the past.

Most of us go through life trying to avoid situations that cause us fear or anxiety. Who wants to be thinking about the bottomless abyss all the time? But who ever really forgets it either? Most of what we do in life, the way we organize our days, choose our work and our friends and our hobbies, sedate and excite ourselves, search for faith or decide we don't need one, all this is a reflection of the ways in which we avoid and pursue our preoccupation with the abyss. The abyss is not simply death, or limits to our understanding, although that is the way some have defined it. The abyss is the reality that frightens us, yet possesses, paradoxically, that which can comfort and uphold us as well.

This is a subject so primal it belongs mainly in children's stories. In the story I read today, Little Bear becomes aware of the darkness, and it frightens him so much he can't sleep. Conventional solutions don't work. No matter how many lanterns light up the house, it's still dark outside.

It's the same for us. We have our ways of pretending it's not dark outside. We need them, to be sure, but they can never completely fool us into believing it is day when it is really night. And as Jim Finley says, "During the day the things that are close to us are clear and visible. [But]...in the dark night of faith we find our ego-self stumbling about over itself, lost to all that was reassuring and familiar." Once you are aware of the dark, you need something more than a lantern. You need faith.

We skeptics often think that religious faith is concocted of speculations about realities we cannot know or experience. So we doubt its merit. But true faith is something we *can* know or experience. When Big Bear finally carries Little Bear *out into the dark itself,* Little Bear learns what night is, and letting go of his fear, falls asleep. Night is not unknowable. The darkness *is* all around us, bright with moon and stars, and we are held, securely, in loving arms.

It's the same truth in rowing. You cannot learn how to move *on* the water until you have fallen *in.* Or at least, I couldn't. Then that's how I remembered what faith is. It's an individual truth that reminds us we are not alone.

Most of us gathered here today have not been able to get by on the conventional assurances of religious faith. We hold on to what we know and can experience, and if that is not enough, then, tough. We'll manage anyway.

But we are not really so different from other people. The darkness is all around everyone, at night. Yet we seem to be willing to live without the insights, the moon, or the stars of night; without letting ourselves go to sleep, secure of the loving arms that are also around each of us. And that seems like a lot to be missing.

One of the lessons I learned this summer from rowing is that there are many ways to approach faith. You can find it anytime you are willing to fall in. You can fall in the water, or you can fall in love, or you can fall into the abyss. You can venture out into the night, the "dark night of faith," as Jim Finley calls it, and find what has eluded you for so long.

T.S. Eliot wrote, "In order to arrive at what you do not know / You must go by a way which is the way of ignorance." You must experience the paradox, fall into the bottomless abyss, to learn that the unending center will hold you, and there is nothing to fear. How you will do that depends on who you are. But the paradox and the truth are the same for everyone. Fall, and the center will hold you.

Some of the people in my rowing class have moved on to the larger, eight-person boats. I saw them out on the water this week. But I don't think I'll be doing that. I plan to stay with the single shell, just me and my anxiety and the water, working on my stroke, with my rowing buddy, I hope, not too far away. Being out there on my own helps me to remember what I've learned. It was a long time, too long, since I had fallen anywhere. I don't ever want to forget how much I need to.

We all need to. However individual, or idiosyncratic the way we find it, our faith is, as Jim Finley has written, "an obscure vision of the secret of our own deepest self." It is obscure, because we see it in the dark. It is secret, because we conceal it under layers of coping and self-deception and avoidance of the truth that darkness is all around us, and we are safe and at home in it. But there is no abyss too deep, no darkness too menacing, no water too murky to keep us from the promise of faith. When we find our own way to it, we will know that it is real. We *will* find our own way to it, because faith will find us-- wherever and whenever we fall in. And when we do, the center will hold us, and all fear will melt into the knowledge that we are secure as we can be day or night.

Resources used to prepare this sermon include T.S. Eliot, "East Coker" in *Four Quartets* (New York: Harcourt, Brace & World, Inc., 1943); James Finley, *Merton's Palace of Nowhere: A Search for God through Awareness of the True Self* (Notre Dame, Indiana: Ave Maria Press, 1978); and Martin Waddell, *Can't You Sleep, Little Bear?* (Cambridge, Massachusetts: Candlewick Press, 1992).

TAKING FUN SERIOUSLY

March 14, 2004

The small gallery on Main Street that shows the work of designers Charles and Ray Eames does not overtly lend itself to spiritual reflection. The reverence there is for design--the furniture, textiles, photography and films that comprise the life work of these two talented artists. There's a sense of quiet industry going on in the back room behind the display; but they welcome you even if you just want to look. I've been in there several times. Each time I've noticed that inscribed on the wall over the front door are the words "We don't take fun seriously enough." That exhortation, combined with the cheerful fabrics, and quirky, iconic chairs, always gives me pause. Perhaps Charles and Ray Eames want us to know that good design is fun, and that fun is too important in life not to take seriously. Beauty gives pleasure. We create it to enjoy ourselves.

Creation and enjoyment are also linked in subtle, revealing hints we find in ancient scripture, among other places. "This is the day which the Lord has made," wrote the psalmist. What to do with the day? Not work--not war--not striving of any kind; just "rejoice and be glad."

The contemporary, earth-centered vision of Annie Dillard makes a similar point: "We are here to abet creation and to witness to it," she writes, "so that creation need not play to an empty house." To be alive is to enjoy the day and the specific and personal ways in which the world reveals itself to us. In one sense, it is all we are asked to do with our lives.

Yet most of us find it difficult. The experience of pleasure for its own sake does not come naturally. And we don't take it seriously enough, though life without it is cheerless and dull. All my adult life I have associated happiness with productivity. I say, find work you enjoy, do it conscientiously, and you will be fulfilled. Even though ministry is one of the least quantifiable activities imaginable, and progress in churches happens about as quickly as plate tectonic shifts, I do make myself happy toiling away, measuring my output by standards that are difficult to describe.

Recreation is a lot like work for many of us. We prefer fun to be productive too, instead of something to do simply because it gives us pleasure. If it is good for you--if it produces an ancillary benefit--it is somehow more valuable than fun just for its own sake. We all rejoice when something we love, like red wine or chocolate, turns out to be good for our health. We are uneasy, even guilty, about pleasure. Think about it. When was the last time you had fun? If it's been a while, it's time to take it more seriously.

Fun doesn't have to be dangerous, take us far from home, or require us to step out of character. But if we don't take it seriously enough, we won't have much fun, and that is truly sad. There is something about the things we do for no other reason than pure enjoyment--whether listening to music, or looking at a beautiful painting, or exploring a part of the world we have never seen, or growing things in the garden--the list could go on and on; there is something about such activity that is essential and spiritual and connected to the simple fact of being alive.

One of my most vivid childhood memories is of my older brother, who stopped on the way to school one day, picked up a piece of pretty blue glass off the street, and immediately sat down on the curb to look through it. I was walking with him, but I got tired of waiting, so I went on ahead. Later I heard that the school had to send someone out to get him because he sat there for a long time, and was late.

Wonder is fun. It is everywhere. Just think about the new pictures this week that show us almost all the way to the beginning of the universe. If you look up at the night sky, it's out there past Orion.

While I was getting ready to write my sermon the other day, I went out with my dog and stopped to talk to a neighbor. She told me she once had a dog who liked to be vacuumed. Though most dogs I know would not find that enjoyable, I smile to think of one creature's sensual preference.

Physical pleasure is fun.
Movement is fun.
Cooking is fun.

Music is fun.

Once you think about it, the list can grow quite long.

And if fun doesn't come easily, we should work at it. The little mouse in the Arnold Lobel fable sets forth on a trip to the seashore. He overcomes fear and danger along the way; even loses his tail. But when he arrives at his destination, the beauty of the ocean and the colors of the sunset fill him with deep peace and contentment.

Spalding Gray worked hard to find his Perfect Moment. He postponed his return home from a trip to Thailand, just so that he could have one. Such experiences can only become more elusive as we grow more desperate, but he was lucky. As he bobbed up and down in the Indian Ocean, drifting dangerously out to sea, oblivious to the depths, the sharks, and the friends calling to him from shore, he too found himself at peace. And his Perfect Moment came to him.

But it doesn't always. When I planned this sermon, I expected to be refreshed from our trip to Madrid, full of stories about how to have fun in Spain. As it turned out, our vacation was not all that much fun. The weather was horrible: cold and rainy; David was sick for a couple of days; my brother left me a cryptic phone message midweek, saying, "Don't worry, but Mom's in the hospital." The trip began to feel like something to survive, rather than the carefree sunny holiday we had anticipated. Of course, there are many wonderful things to do in Madrid even when the weather is bad, and we bucked ourselves up, stopped complaining, and did them all. In the end, there were even a few close to Perfect Moments.

Now the bombings in Madrid have cast a pall over everything. Our disappointment about our vacation seems terribly selfish, compared to the anguish of the people there. In a world that has gone so violently awry, the quest for fun becomes trivial and off the mark. It's another sign that we don't take fun seriously enough, that we have let the world become so scary.

Creation has become an arena for humankind's deadly conflicts, not a garden to enjoy. We do little to subdue our destructive bent, even less to nurture our yearning for peace. Bombed-out grieving cities are not places where people have fun. To have fun, people must be at peace. We don't take fun seriously enough. If we did, the world would be a very different place.

We all know that it is good to take care of ourselves, to change pace and relax, to enjoy simple, healthy pleasures. But fun is not something we do simply for ourselves. To take fun seriously is to take the whole of creation into account, and to think about our place in it.

To enjoy life--to witness and abet creation, as Annie Dillard put it, is the human vocation on this earth. Our role is to appreciate the beautiful world that touches every one of our senses with delight. Our work is to help it flourish. Our days are the time we are given to nurture this place in which we live, and if we are so inclined, to make something beautiful for it.

It's paradoxical, but taking fun seriously can make us feel a little sad. We haven't lived up to our promise as humans, nor do we enjoy life as much as we could. Yes, life can be challenging, even tragic, and no one is left untouched by its rigors. The Perfect Moments are few and far between. Sometimes they elude us completely. Even so, there is so much more we could have, if only we could take in this great gift of each and every day; if only we could rejoice and be glad. And we can, if we let ourselves have fun, and hurting no one, live in contentment and peace.

Resources used to prepare this sermon include Arnold Lobel, "The Mouse at the Seashore" in *Fables* (New York: HarperCollins, 1980). Annie Dillard is cited in *Singing in the Living Tradition*, No. 420 (Boston: Beacon Press, 1993). The story about Spalding Gray's search for the Perfect Moment can be found in *Swimming To Cambodia* (New York: Theater Communications Group, 1985) and in the film by the same name. The Eames Gallery is on Main Street, Santa Monica.

A PILGRIM'S POSTCARDS

August 8, 2004

Neighborhood Church, Pasadena, CA

We all have bad travel stories to tell. A few of mine come to mind: an impulsive, pointless, ill-advised midnight trip to Atlantic City in a borrowed car when I was a college sophomore; a lonely weekend surrounded by honeymooning couples at a Bermuda resort; a night in Laguna Beach interrupted by the arrest made in the room next door. I've been stalked in Paris and poisoned by mesquite in Hawaii. And I've gotten lost almost everywhere I've ever been.

I'm not a naturally adventurous person. As travel has become both more difficult and more fraught with fear these past few years, I've had to work on myself to take pleasure in moving around the world. When worry makes me hesitate to take a trip, I remind myself of what I discover wherever I go: a pilgrim has a better time than a tourist.

That discovery has made all the difference to me. Pilgrims and tourists are not so different from each other in many ways. They both venture into unfamiliar territory. Unlike Antoine de Saint-Exupéry's distinction between a geographer and an explorer, they both leave home. The same sights pass before their jet-lagged eyes. And yet--the differences are dramatic.

A tourist goes places, but a pilgrim has an experience. Each can take the same trip, but the pilgrim will see something no postcard can depict. The pilgrim undergoes a transformation, inside and out, wherever the journey leads. This glimmering of transcendence that comes with a pilgrim's journey puts fears and inconveniences into perspective, and opens the door to revelation.

This was never more clear to me than in Rome, a pilgrimage destination if there ever was one. Pilgrims are everywhere, doing dramatic things. At the Scala Santa--the Holy Staircase, at the Basilica of St. John of Lateran, eager devotees ascend the marble steps on their knees. Elsewhere, pilgrims cross thresholds of churches and catacombs, awestruck and rapt with appreciation not only for the beautiful art works adorning these spaces, but also for the experience of being in the spaces themselves: sacred spaces, where the holy is real.

It's been four years since I spent a month of study leave in Rome, but these images are still fresh: how the Jubilee Year 2000 drew pilgrims from all over the world, eager to pray and to confess and to breathe in the air of the great sacred places of their faith. That's not why I was there, however. I went to Rome on a pilgrimage of another kind: to walk in the footsteps of Margaret Fuller, the American journalist, literary critic, and Transcendentalist friend of Ralph Waldo Emerson who got caught up in the revolutionary movement for an Italian republic.

Still, I crossed paths with many of the Roman Catholic pilgrims and saw a great many churches along the way. We may not have had much in common other than our sojourn in that magnificent city, and the basic expectation that every pilgrim carries: that this trip will somehow change us.

Mary Morris, traveling by train across Poland, realizes that her trip--one of many--is a death and a rebirth, the end of her childhood as she anticipates a baby of her own. She remembers that her grandmother was buried alive as a child, in a place not too far from there. This grim bit of history jumps to her own childhood, which had some of the joy squeezed out of it by demanding parents, and laid the foundation for quite a few lonely years as a young adult. What goes on inside Mary Morris during that train trip, as she returns home to her husband and the arrival of their baby, is what all pilgrims seek: a journey that gives new life.

According to scholars of religion, a pilgrimage is a journey to a sacred place, which has the unique property of allowing the traveler to cross over from the every day world to the transcendent one. Every religious tradition has its sacred places: the basilicas and tombs of the Catholic faith; the city of Banaras, where Hindus go to seek moksha, or release; Jerusalem, Mecca, Lhasa. Even the secular world has its shrines: Graceland, the home of Elvis Presley; the monuments and memorials of our nation's capital; Ellis Island and Plymouth Rock. People go there, hoping to see and learn something that will change their lives in some way.

My own pilgrimage to Rome was not a conventional religious one, but the places I visited were more meaningful, if not exactly sacred, because they were part of Margaret Fuller's life and landscape. Where she lived, worked, and walked were not simply tourist attractions for me. They were places that gave me a glimpse of what the world looked like to her--to cross over into her reality and try to imagine what it was like to be her in it. Seeking to know her world as I read her letters and newspaper articles, and history of the Roman Republic, gave me a sense of her life I could have acquired in no other way.

Along the way, I began asking myself, why was I so interested in this person? I imagine we were quite different temperamentally. And yet as I came to know her--and not just know about her--I gained some new insights into myself. The qualities that intrigued me in Margaret Fuller--her gutsy, almost combative personality, her incisive, critical mind--were not ones I shared; the risks she took, I would not take; the fate she met, I would hope to avoid.

If I came back from Rome changed in any way, it was in the depth of my self-knowledge as much as in the amount of information I had gathered about Margaret Fuller. And self-knowledge is a valuable outcome for any trip. Just as travel writer Mary Morris returns home from her epic adventure from Beijing to Berlin, aware of a new life growing inside her, we would all like to feel something new after going somewhere different. We would come home having observed not only the novel details of others' lives in other places, but new facts about our own. Self-knowledge is good, even transforming, but it is not sacred in the traditional religious sense. A traditional pilgrimage brings the traveler to a holy place. Simply having made it there is life-changing.

Diana Eck, a scholar of religion and authority on Hinduism, describes a holy place as a portal to the transcendent. In the Hindu tradition, it is where the gods once made themselves known to human devotees. The country of India is saturated with religious activity, and it has a sacred geography. Holy places overlay the land. Every place and every journey to it have more than one meaning, mundane and sacred.

My trip to Rome was different from other trips I've taken

because my quest for Margaret Fuller overlaid the city with her geography. A city apartment building had layers of meaning: that she lived there, and that she lived there when she was pregnant with her lover's child, and that she came and went from that place knowing that she would never be accepted at home in New England ever again, and that she could look out the window and see history being made. The layers of life and meaning imposed on the places I saw may not have made them holy places, but they gave them something a pilgrim hopes to find: a sense of the world as a place of revelation. No gods appeared on the Via Del Corso. But the world looks different to me because I stopped and paid my respects to the place where a woman lived and loved and left her mark on history.

The world is a place of revelation. Wherever we go, it shows us an opening to an experience of life we just might miss if we are only tourists. Tourists see the things that are there, but they do not look for the layers of meaning, the relationships between their own lives and those they observe, the geography of interconnection that weaves us together as one.

Anthropologists have studied the sense of community that pilgrims experience on their journeys. Because pilgrims leave home and enter unfamiliar terrain, and are uprooted and a little lost, the usual rules and norms don't apply; relationships alter, and a new, idealistic society forms for those who travel together. Among the devout, the context shifts from daily life to sacred time, and everything that happens in sacred time is sacred. The experience of community is profound under these conditions, leaving participants yearning for more. And all people yearn for something like it, even if they never leave home.

People seek experiences such as pilgrimages to have an intense experience of community, to feel what it's like to be in the world and not to be alone, to be bonded to each other in a sacred time and place. To live in the world as a pilgrim is to search for this intense experience of community, its intimacy and its grace, whether the threshold we cross is in Banares, India, or in Pasadena, California. It does not matter where you step through the doorway; what matters is what you are seeking when you do.

To look at the whole world as a place of revelation, its geography as sacred, its people as guides to our own true selves, that is what it is to be a pilgrim on this vast and strange planet. It is to seek the layers of life and meaning that lend depth and a glimpse of eternity to what we see to meet each other on the way; to be together in sacred time. We can do that here; we can do that now; if we live as pilgrims.

Resources used to prepare this sermon include Mary Morris, *Wall to Wall: From Beijing to Berlin by Rail* (New York: Doubleday, 1991); and lecture notes from Diana Eck, "Religious Rituals," Harvard University, 1978.

COMMUNITY LIFE

May 19, 2002

Any Sunday I'm not in church in Santa Monica, wherever I might happen to be, I'm always thinking about what you are doing here. A lifetime of church going, compounded by being a minister, has permanently conditioned me. I don't really feel at home anywhere on a Sunday morning except in church, preferably here, but sometimes almost anywhere else will do.

This Easter Sunday David and I roamed around Singapore until we found the English-speaking service at the Anglican church there. The rituals were confusing and we were hot and out of place, but it still felt right to be there. I remembered that on Easter two years earlier, in Rome on a similar study leave, we had huddled with the throngs outside St. Peter's just to be part of the church action. When I asked, "I wonder what they're doing in Santa Monica right now," I realized of course that it wasn't time for church at home and you were all probably fast asleep.

I did not expect to learn much about Unitarian Universalism on this trip. In Bali, where we spent most of our time, nearly everyone practices a local form of Hinduism that is quite different from the Indian religion I studied in school. There are no Unitarian Universalist churches there, which to be honest was one of the reasons why we went--looking for something totally different, a fresh perspective on everything.

On the surface, we Unitarian Universalists have practically nothing in common with the Balinese. Elaborate, colorful rituals dominate Balinese life. Every village--even a village as small as three hundred people--has three temples. The temples require ceremonies. The people always seem to be preparing for, celebrating, or cleaning up after a ceremony. They make us look drab and ritually deprived.

Despite these contrasts, interesting similarities did emerge. Before long, I could see how we share certain distinctive values. The Balinese practice religious tolerance and welcome outsiders into their ceremonies and culture. As one young man explained to us, the Balinese believe that people have many different ideas of God, and that all are equally valid. What draws people together in religious community is ritual and relationship, not dogma.

The rituals require tremendous skill--the offerings alone are works of art and belong to a rich culture in which everyone is an artist. After a while the outsider can see that this religious activity--as exotic as it may appear, is actually inseparable from daily life. Even the most traditional rituals contain quirky modern elements. We attended one ceremony with a young family who brought the usual carefully assembled offerings of food, along with a small woven tray containing a cell phone. I had the honor of offering that tray, which was returned with its contents after the temple priest had blessed it.

Balinese religion is much like ours in the sense that it is about the way they live from day to day. It is about food and art and family and work. It is about having a place to go. But most of all, it is about community. Rituals weave people together in a symbolic activity to show--consciously and unconsciously--that community is life.

I found myself thinking about our church quite often there, perhaps because we visited so many temples. Sometimes I thought, "I wonder what they are doing now." Most of the time, I just thought about the meaning of our community and how different life would be for me--for any of us--without it.

The Balinese cannot imagine life without community. I questioned our guides quite closely about village customs and governance. Each village governs itself and anyone living there can participate--even foreigners, if they are interested.

They make their decisions by consensus. Sometimes it takes a long time to make a decision. Since every village must have three temples, their building meetings would probably be long even by Unitarian Universalist standards. Fortunately for them temple designs are according to strict tradition--few decisions ever need to be made. Another village tradition concerns belonging. In Bali, you can never leave your village. You can move away, go to work in Jakarta or San Francisco. But the village still considers you to be a member--a non-participating member--but spiritually, very much present.

This way of looking at membership is essential because when you die, your body must go back to your village. "You cannot quit your village," one Balinese man told me, "because then you would have no one to cremate you." Cremation is the single most important and essential ritual in Hindu life. It takes a village to have one.

Your community remains your home forever. It is life and it is also death. Its scope is limitless; its gate is always open. By our standards of voluntary association, this is a level of community that comes close to a nearly suffocating inescapability. Perhaps it does for some Balinese as well--we didn't meet them; they are probably in Jakarta or San Francisco. And yet there is a sense of acceptance, of being held and protected that is very compelling and--in more ways than one--very hard to leave behind.

Every style of community is different. But it springs from the same human need to affiliate with others because life is not the same without it. In the Jewish story I told earlier for our meditation, the rabbi teaches that night is over and day begins when one human being can look into the face of another and say, "This is my brother; this is my sister." This kind of daylight is life itself. Life asks us to acknowledge the reality of our kinship with one another.

Here in this community, whatever our individual needs or social skills or marital status, affirming our kinship is central to our faith. Even if all you want or need to do is come and sit in this sanctuary with other people on a Sunday morning, you are participating in community. We are all different in the sense that some of us need to spend a lot of time together, others of us not so much. Membership embraces a diverse array of behaviors, but its meaning is universal. We need each other to live.

Scientist E.O. Wilson has written frequently about life and human nature. In his most recent book, *The Future of Life*, he writes about the human need for community. "Each of us finds a comfortable position," Wilson observes, "somewhere along the continuum that ranges from complete withdrawal and self-absorption at one end to full civic engagement and reciprocity at the other. The position is never fixed. We fret, vacillate, and steer our lives through the riptide of countervailing instincts that press from both ends of the continuum. The uncertainty we feel is not a curse. It is not a confusion on the road out of Eden. It is just the human condition. We are intelligent mammals, fitted by evolution--by God, if you prefer--to pursue personal ends through cooperation."

The four naughty boys in the Balinese children's story learned early in life that strength comes from standing together. Like the bundle of wood their father holds, they cannot break if they are joined to one another. But as Wilson has pointed out, there is no one fixed way to be together: throughout our lives, we constantly adjust how close and how far we need to be from one another. There are many ways to connect and to belong. Even when we are far away.

In our world, church members do move away, and others join us. Whatever time we have together is precious and helps us to grow strong. These hours we are gathered together stand for something that cannot change, even if we move far away. Wherever we go, we are still connected to one another.

When I am far away, my wondering what you are all doing here is not so much an inability to stop thinking about work, but a way of remembering how important you are to me--to my life. This community we gather together each Sunday--and convene in smaller groups throughout the week--carries a power that is greater than any of us can know on our own. We are the bundle of wood. We are woven together in the web of creation. We are the home we make together, because we are life itself.

Resources used to prepare this sermon include Edward O. Wilson, *The Future of Life* (New York: Alfred A. Knopf, 2002); and "The Four Naughty Boys," Victor Mason with Gillian Bell, *Balinese Children's Favorite Stories* (Singapore: Periplus Editions, 2001).

THE WORD

March 7, 1999

One of my favorite writers and spoken word performers, Jim Carroll, makes an appearance in Santa Monica about once a year, and I try to have tickets to hear him. Not that tickets are all that difficult to obtain. Not many people have heard of him, and though the film version of his teenage memoirs, *The Basketball Diaries*, did boost his popularity briefly, I have usually had to talk someone into going with me.

Jim Carroll is unpredictable, but always interesting. The last time I went to hear him was no exception. The odd and diverse group of people who regularly show up to listen to Jim Carroll gathered in the small theater at McCabe's Guitar Shop. It was the usual less than capacity crowd. There we sat and waited for over an hour, while McCabe's manager would occasionally pop onto the stage and tell us that Jim was late, but would be there soon.

So we waited, patient as sheep, never complaining or showing any restlessness. We were seasoned Jim Carroll fans, used to the delays, the good days and the bad. More time passed.

The audience drifted into a resigned, almost meditative state, but no one left. Eventually the exasperated manager came back on stage and informed us that the show was cancelled, that was the last time McCabe's would ever book Jim Carroll, and we could all get our money back. So we all trooped upstairs, got our refunds, and scattered into the night.

No one was angry. Rather we acted like devotees of a capricious spiritual teacher whose words were precious, like moments of grace, not for the asking, but gratefully received whenever they might be bestowed. Not until David questioned whether we were simply slavish fans did it occur to me that my attitude was somehow inflated.

All my life I have been mesmerized and transported by the spoken word. I grew up in suburban New Jersey, where an entire generation of teenagers listened, every night, to Jean Shepherd spin tales of his Indiana adolescence on WOR radio station. I fell asleep listening, my transistor radio pressed up to my ear, caught up in the power of memoir and story. If you think this was an isolated instance of behavior, I suggest you take a look at the Jean Shepherd web site, where that same generation of listeners, now turned 50 and full of nostalgia, have collected their own stories about those radio shows and how they shaped their youth. How all that listening has shaped me must be obvious as I stand here, speaking, having chosen the word as my own organizing principle and life work. And while Jim Carroll and Jean Shepherd are not religious teachers within our tradition, and are only two small examples of those who have used the spoken word effectively, memorably, even transcendently; they taught me how powerful and sacred the word can be.

In the beginning was the Word and the Word was with God and the Word was God. In the Gospel according to John, the Word is more than something spoken. The Word--*logos* is the Greek word the author uses--is the inner thought and reason, an intuitive source of truth. It comes from God, has a life of its own, and conveys holiness through its power. The Word is an instrument of God's presence in life, according to John, and that is why the word became flesh in the person of Jesus.

Our world is deeply affected by the word. The Christian tradition has given us one story of its holiness and its transforming power. There are others too. The American Black folktale, "How Nehemiah Got Free," recounts how a clever slave secured his freedom with the power of his words. First he had to meet his match, the cruel slave owner who boasted he could outwit him. But Nehemiah was ready with a verbal volley so fast and so well placed that he won his freedom in one round. "True is true," reflects the narrator of the tale. And freedom is right.

The word brings forth the power of truth used for freedom, dignity and justice. Nehemiah used it to good effect, and so have others who have been oppressed. Having the freedom to speak is a basic right that some people have not been allowed to exercise. To listen to those who have not been heard is itself a powerful act of social change.

Latina [women] theologians use a striking phrase--*permítanme hablar*--allow me to speak--to insist on speaking and being heard. Ada María Isasi-Díaz writes in her book, *Mujerista Theology*, "We have never been absent from history but we have been ignored by historical accounts. Therefore, our insistence on speaking, on making known our histories ...lends force and sustenance to our positions, refuses to compromise or equivocate, learns from failures, and knows (by experience) that it has the capability of overcoming every obstacle, even repression itself."

The spoken word has "the capability of overcoming every obstacle." There is no more powerful tool of justice and transformation. That is why those who have been denied it make speech the organizing principle of their struggle for liberation. "When Latinas use the phrase 'permítanme hablar,'" Isasi-Díaz writes, "we are asking for a respectful silence from all those who have the power to set up definitions of what it is to be human, a respectful silence so others can indeed hear our cries denouncing oppression and injustice, so others can understand our vision of a just society. We know that if those with power do not hear us, they will give no credence to the full humanity of Latinas. That is why we insist on the capacity of Hispanic women to speak our own word. For Latinas to speak and to be heard is what makes it possible for us to attest to our own humanity."

The power of the word, whoever the speaker, is that it makes it possible for us "to attest to our own humanity." In attesting to our humanity, we overcome the obstacles of injustice and oppression. The word makes us free.

In the beginning was the Word. Not just at the beginning of time, as John suggests, but at the beginning of every human life. Eudora Welty remembers learning the alphabet, which she first saw as enchanted illuminations in her children's story books, "a part of the word's beauty and holiness that had been there from the start." Kathleen Norris writes about how a human infant begins to build a vocabulary at the age of one month, baby steps towards what later becomes a great leap of faith, to say "yes" to life itself.

She remembers a college professor telling her that "our words are wiser than we are," as if the capacity to use words reaches inside to sources that are deeper, smarter and more truthful than we usually manage to be.

That is why words are powerful. They "attest to our humanity" by speaking universal truths we have known since the beginning of time. "Language used truly, not mere talk, neither propaganda, nor chatter," Kathleen Norris writes, "has real power. Its words are allowed to be themselves, to bless or curse, wound or heal. They have the power of a 'word made flesh,' of ordinary speech that suddenly takes hold, causing listeners to pay close attention," perhaps even to grow or change in some way, because they have heard something that teaches them truth and they know it.

When I happened upon the Jean Shepherd web site, I was impressed that his fans had amassed tapes of his shows--more than twenty years' worth, interviews, biography, even his current mailing address. But that was not all. The fans had gathered their own stories about listening to him late at night.

What was powerful about Jean Shepherd's monologues was not simply what he said, but what we heard. Something in his stories about growing up in that small Indiana town spoke the truth to those of us growing up in New Jersey. Young listeners pressed their ears to their transistor radios and knew that they were not alone.

The word is the truth when we listen to each other and hear the voice of common human experience. The word is power if the truth moves us to act towards each other in recognition of our bond. The word is personal, speaking in terms of one life experience or another, telling us about growing up in Indiana, but teaching us about growing up in New Jersey. The word is universal, leading us from the particular truth of one life to the common truth of all life.

To speak the word is to reach inside to sources that are deeper, smarter, and more truthful than we realized we could be. To listen to the word--especially to the word of people who ask to be heard to attest to their humanity--is to bring truth, freedom and justice to life together. The word overcomes every obstacle in its way.

While I was preparing this sermon, whenever I got stuck in my writing I would take another look at the Jean Shepherd website. Yes, and I admit I looked at the Jim Carroll website too. You can see a snapshot of the house where Jean Shepherd grew up in Hammond, Indiana. You can read a list of Jim Carroll's upcoming tour appearances--but don't count on them.

But you cannot hear the power of the word by reading *about* these people. You can only hear it by listening to them. Even then--

these two might not have much to say to you. But someone does, and you do. You can speak the word too. In fact you do, every time your words attest to your humanity and speak the truth of who you are. Only you can speak for yourself, though every one of us can listen. Think about how much better we would know each other if we could speak that way more often and know that someone would listen.

When you speak the truth of who you are you are drawing on the power of all that is within you, the source that is deeper, smarter, and more honest than you ever realized you could be. That is the word, and it removes all obstacles. Listen to someone speak the Word and learn you are not alone. Speak the truth and hear it and let the power of the Word make you free.

Resources used to prepare this sermon include Ada Maria Isasi-Díaz, *Mujerista Theology* (Maryknoll, NY: Orbis Books, 1996); Kathleen Norris, *Amazing Grace: A Vocabulary of Faith* (New York: Riverhead Books, 1998); "How Nehemiah Got Free" in *The People Could Fly: American Black Folktales*, ed. Virginia Hamilton (New York: Knopf, 1985); and Eudora Welty, *One Writer's Beginnings* (Cambridge: Harvard University Press, 1998).